Computing Fundamentals

Lotus® 1-2-3®, Release 2.01/2.2

Donald L. Byrkett
Miami University, Oxford, Ohio

▲ Addison-Wesley Publishing Company

Reading, Massachusetts • Menlo Park, California • New York
Don Mills, Ontario • Wokingham, England • Amsterdam • Bonn
Sydney • Singapore • Tokyo • Madrid • San Juan

This book was produced by the Addison-Wesley Electronic Production Department on an Apple Macintosh II with PageMaker. The output was generated on an Apple LaserWriter II NTX.

This book is in the Addison-Wesley *Computing Fundamentals Series*.
Series Editor: William S. Davis Allen County Public Library
Ft. Wayne, Indiana

The books in Addison-Wesley's *Computing Fundamentals Series* feature tutorials that teach the reader how to use specific software packages. Their low selling price makes them attractive as self-teaching aids and as supplements to a primary text. A unique feature entitled "What can go wrong?" anticipates problems, suggests a cause, and helps the reader recover. The modular nature of the series should prove attractive to the instructor of a miocrocomputer applications course. Current and planned titles include:

Lotus® 1-2-3® Release 2.01/2.2	PageMaker® for the Macintosh
Concepts, Second Edition	Pagemaker® for the IBM PC
dBASE III PLUS™	PC-DOS & MS-DOS®
dBASE IV™	UNIX® Systems
Microsoft® Word 5.0	WordPerfect® 5.0/5.1

Lotus and 1-2-3 are registered trademarks of Lotus Development Corporation.

Library of Congress Cataloging-in-Publication Data
Byrkett, Donald L.
    Computing fundamentals: Lotus 1-2-3, release 2.01/2.2 / Donald L.
Byrkett.
        p. cm.
    ISBN 0-201-52474-0
    1. Lotus 1-2-3 (Computer program) 2. Business--Data processing.
3. Electronic spreadsheets. I. Title.
HF5548.4.L67B97   1990   90-35673
650'.0285'5369--dc20   CIP

    5 6 7 8 9 10 AL 9594939291

Preface

Computing Fundamentals: Lotus 1-2-3 is a part of Addison-Wesley's *Computing Fundamentals Series*. Its purpose is to teach you how to use 1-2-3, one of today's most popular electronic spreadsheet programs. Except for elementary typing skills, it assumes no prior knowledge.

Getting started with an electronic spreadsheet program can be a difficult task. Often, the only available resource is the reference manual. Though the 1-2-3 Reference Manual is well written, it is intended for experienced users, not beginners.

Because it is so popular, many books have been written about 1-2-3. Some read like reference manuals. Others focus on advanced features designed to take experienced 1-2-3 users beyond the manual. A few *are* aimed at beginners, but most of them are quite expensive. This book was written to provide a low cost, introductory book that quickly teaches you how to use 1-2-3 effectively.

Computing Fundamentals: Lotus 1-2-3 does not cover every 1-2-3 feature; that is not its intent. Instead, it introduces the fundamental features you'll need to create, modify, and print spreadsheets, to display and print graphs, and to sort and query a worksheet database. The book is designed to provide an introduction to 1-2-3 using either Release 2.01 or the newer Release 2.2. All of the keystroke instructions will work exactly the same using either release. All of the screens displayed in the tutorials are as they would appear in Release 2.2; in some cases, there will be slight differences in the appearance of Release 2.01 screens. The tutorials cover some features of Release 2.2 that are not available in Release 2.01. This is noted in the text and you may skip over this material without a loss in continuity. When you finish, you'll have sufficient background to read the 1-2-3 Reference Manual and learn additional features on your own.

Like the other books in the series, *Computing Fundamentals: Lotus 1-2-3* is organized as a set of tutorials. Many tutorials assume the reader will follow the instructions perfectly and that *nothing* will go wrong. That's unrealistic; in the real world, something always seems to go wrong, and nothing is more frustrating to the beginner than hitting a dead end. Appearing throughout this book is a unique feature entitled "What can go wrong?" that anticipates problems, suggests a cause, and tells you how to recover. You should find it very useful.

Acknowledgments

I'd like to thank Mr. William Davis, the series editor, for inviting me to write this book and for helping me to formulate a writing style appropriate for a beginning user. Comments and suggestions from the following reviewers also proved very useful: Professor Janice Esposito of Quinnipiac College, Professor Paul Higbee of the University of North Florida, Professor Fred Homeyer of Angelo State University, Ms. Deborah Lafferty of Addison-Wesley, and Ms. Mary Allyn Webster of the University of Florida.

DLB
Oxford, Ohio

Contents

Electronic
Spreadsheets

This chapter:

- introduces the functions performed by an electronic spreadsheet

- explains basic computer concepts and identifies key hardware and software components

- previews *Computing Fundamentals: Lotus 1-2-3*

Electronic Spreadsheets

Electronic spreadsheet software was one of the first major types of programs to become available for microcomputers. VISICALC, the first electronic spreadsheet program, became available in 1979 and initially ran only on Apple microcomputers. There is a strong correlation between the advent of VISICALC and the initial growth of Apple computer sales. When the IBM PC was introduced in 1981, VISICALC was converted for use on IBM equipment. In 1983, Lotus Development Corporation introduced 1-2-3 for use on the PC. Many people credit the growth of microcomputer usage in business to the availability of these and other early spreadsheet packages.

Sales Projection
Annual growth rate = 10%

Product line	Sales (1000's)			
	Year 1 (Current)	Year 2	Year 3	Year 4
Trucks	$ 750	$ 825	$ 908	$ 998
Cars	3,580	3,938	4,332	4,765
Vans	2,120	2,332	2,565	2,822
Four wheel drive	250	275	303	333
Exports	1,120	1,232	1,355	1,491
Total annual sales	$ 7,820	$ 8,602	$ 9,462	$ 10,408

Figure 1.1 A typical manually created spreadsheet.

Manual Spreadsheets

Before the introduction of electronic spreadsheets, accountants and other business analysts used manual spreadsheets to organize information and perform calculations. For example, an analyst might wish to perform a sales projection over the next four years with an annual growth rate of 10% (Fig. 1.1). The analyst would take a sheet of paper (or a columnar tablet) and list the major product lines down the left edge of the paper, forming a row for each product. Four columns would be used to display the sales figures for each year. Sales for the current year would be listed in column 1 for each product. Using a calculator and the 10% growth rate, the analyst would calculate the sales figures for each product in each successive year. Column totals would also be calculated to provide total annual sales figures.

However, developing these tables manually presents some problems. They are subject to calculation errors, since the calculations are performed manually by entering the numbers in a calculator. Data entry errors are also easy to make. The tables often require revision or updating. In the above example, new products might be added or new projections might be required as each year passes. These updates require developing the spreadsheet all over again. Finally, analysts often wish to calculate the same spreadsheet under different sets of assumptions. In the above example, the analyst might wish to perform the same projection with a 5% growth rate. This would require recalculating the entire spreadsheet.

Electronic Spreadsheets

Electronic spreadsheets duplicate the functions of manual spreadsheets but overcome many of their shortcomings. Electronic spreadsheets provide increased calculation accuracy, easy updating, and the ability to recalculate column and row totals quickly under different sets of assumptions. With electronic spreadsheets, formulas are used that, once verified, may be used over and over with a high degree of accuracy. Electronic spreadsheets may be modified and updated easily as situations change. Columns and rows may be added, deleted, or rearranged. Data elements and formulas may be changed. Finally, electronic spreadsheets are recalculated automatically when any numbers are modified. This allows the analyst to evaluate a series of business scenarios or growth rates by simply reentering certain numbers in the spreadsheet.

Today, most electronic spreadsheet programs provide enhanced capabilities such as graphing, data management and retrieval, and custom programming. **Graphing capability** allows a user to select certain columns or rows of the spreadsheet to be displayed visually as a bar chart, pie chart, or plot. **Data management and retrieval capability** allows the user to treat the spreadsheet as a database in which the rows represent records and the columns represent fields. This allows the spreadsheet user to search for records containing certain types of information and to reorder or sort the records in the spreadsheet. Many spreadsheet programs allow **custom programming or macro capability**, which allows many functions to be performed by writing a sequence of steps that may be executed by giving a single command. In addition, many other capabilities are provided, including the possibility of combining several spreadsheets, the creation of spreadsheets with three or more dimensions, enhancing the appearance of a printed spreadsheet, and the use of functions to perform mathematical and statistical operations.

Lotus 1-2-3 (generally referred to simply as *1-2-3*) is the most popular electronic spreadsheet on the market. Since its initial release (version 1A), it has been enhanced several times. The current version of 1-2-3 includes most of the enhanced capabilities mentioned above.

Applications

The applications of electronic spreadsheets are countless. Basically, any situation that can be summarized in a table with rows and columns representing different categories can be organized as an electronic spreadsheet. Calculations are easily implemented at each row and column intersection. The more experience you have with spreadsheets, the more creative you'll be in developing applications. Listed below are some possible applications to stimulate your thinking. Potential row and column categories are indicated.

1. Budget (*rows*: budget categories; *columns*: time periods)

2. Economic analysis (*rows*: revenue and cost categories; *columns*: time periods)

3. Inventory (*rows*: stock items; *columns*: characteristics of each item such as stock level, unit cost, target, units on order, and so on)

4. Grade sheet (*rows*: students; *columns*: test and homework results)

5. Batting average calculation (*rows*: possible batting results such as singles, doubles, and so on; *columns*: frequency of each result)

6. Personnel records (*rows*: employees; *columns*: wage and salary information)

7. Income tax calculation (*rows*: line items on tax schedule; *columns*: dollar amount)

8. Mortgage amortization table (*rows*: payment number; *columns*: accumulated interest paid, unpaid principal after each payment, and so on)

9. Experiment results (*rows*: subjects; *columns*: response variable measurements)

10. Mathematics tables (*rows*: argument to function; *columns*: value of function)

The Computer

1-2-3 is an electronic spreadsheet program than runs on IBM PC, PS/2, and compatible computers. (Similar versions are available for other computers, but they will not be covered in this book.) The computer, of course, influences how 1-2-3 works, so it is important that you understand some basic computer concepts before you begin to use 1-2-3. For many readers, the balance of this section will be largely review.

Hardware and Software

The computer system pictured in Fig. 1.2 consists of several components. The keyboard is the primary **input device**. A display unit, or screen, and a printer are common **output devices**. Most systems contain **secondary storage**: one or more floppy disk drives and perhaps a hard disk. The computer links and controls these physical components, which collectively are called **hardware**.

Hardware can do nothing without a program to provide control. A **program** is a set of instructions that guides the computer through a process. Those instructions are stored in the computer's own **memory**.

When you first activate a computer, there is no program in memory. Thus the first step in using the machine is to load a program, usually a special program called the **operating system**. Most microcomputers are designed to automatically read the operating system from disk when they are turned on, a process known as **booting**. Once the operating system is in memory, it can ask the user to type the desired application program's name, read the response, and then load the specified program.

Figure 1.2 A typical computer system. Courtesy of International Business Machines Corporation.

The Screen, Memory, and Secondary Storage

The most common way of communicating with a microcomputer is through the keyboard. When you press a key, a signal flows from the keyboard, through a cable, and into memory, where a code representing the character is stored. Once it is in memory, the character is displayed on the screen. Those two steps happen so quickly that it appears as though you are typing directly to the screen. At first glance, using an electronic spreadsheet really does resemble manually developing a spreadsheet (with the screen representing a table of rows and columns).

However, the analogy quickly breaks down. With the manual approach, data are handwritten or typed directly to paper. With an electronic spreadsheet, data are stored in memory and *then* displayed on the screen. If you turn the screen off, then turn it back on, the data will still be there. If you turn the computer off, then turn it back on, the data will be gone.

The problem is that a computer's memory is **volatile**; in other words, if the machine loses power for any reason, everything stored in memory is lost. That's why **secondary storage** is used. A floppy disk or a hard disk is

nonvolatile; it does not lose its contents when power is cut. To save data, you copy them from main memory to disk. Then, if you should lose power or simply decide to quit working, you can later pick up where you left off simply by telling the computer to copy the data from the disk back into memory.

As you begin to learn any new task, you will make mistakes, and developing spreadsheet applications is no exception. Some errors are trivial and easy to fix. Others, such as losing a complete spreadsheet, can be very discouraging. The easiest way to lose your work is to forget to copy it to disk or to copy it improperly. If you understand the distinction between data on the screen, data in memory, and data on disk, you will be less likely to lose your work.

Getting Ready

The Keyboard

Before you turn to the first tutorial in Chapter 2, briefly preview the equipment and the software you'll be using. Start with the keyboard (Fig. 1.3). To the left of a standard IBM PC keyboard is a set of ten **function keys** labeled F1 through F10. To the right of the keyboard is a numeric keypad; the words and arrows on the bottoms of those keys are for cursor control. (The **cursor** is the flashing underline that indicates the position on the screen where the next character will appear.) On some computers, a device known as a mouse controls the cursor's position.

The center section resembles a typewriter keyboard. A few keys are particularly important. Start with the top row, just to the left of the digit 1,

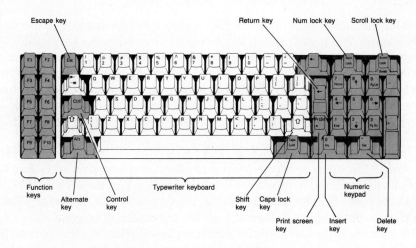

Figure 1.3 Before starting with 1-2-3, familiarize yourself with the keyboard. Shown here is the standard IBM PC keyboard.

where you will see the [Esc], or escape key. Directly under it is the [⇆], or tab key. Continue moving down to the [Ctrl], or control key, a [⇧] or shift key, and the [Alt], or alternate key.

Just to the right of the space bar, still in the bottom row, is the [Caps Lock], or caps lock key. To its right are the [Ins], or insert key, and the [Del], or delete key. Directly above [Caps Lock] is another [⇧] key. To its right is a key marked [PrtSc]; if you simultaneously press [⇧] *and* [PrtSc], a copy of whatever appears on the screen will be printed on the printer. Just above [PrtSc] is the [⏎] key, usually called "return" or "enter." Above [⏎] is the [←], or backspace key. Moving to the right are the [Num Lock], or numeric lock key, and [Scroll Lock], or scroll-lock/break key. Below [Scroll Lock] are the [−] and [+] keys.

The PS/2 keyboard is a bit different (Fig. 1.4). Its twelve function keys are arrayed across the top along with the [Esc], scroll, and pause keys. The typewriter keyboard is at the left; the numeric keypad is at the right; except for the locations of a few keys, they resemble their PC equivalents. The big difference is a bank of cursor control keys located just to the right center of the keyboard.

If you are using an IBM-compatible computer, the layout may be different. Review your keyboard and find the equivalent keys.

Disk Drives

Many microcomputers are equipped with two floppy disk drives. To distinguish them, the left or top one is known as drive A, and the right or bottom one is called drive B. If there is only one floppy disk drive, it is almost always drive A. If the computer has a hard disk, it is usually located inside the computer and is identified as drive C.

Figure 1.4 The keyboard for an IBM PS/2 is different. Courtesy of International Business Machines Corporation.

Program and Data Disks

The tutorial is designed to provide an introduction to Lotus 1-2-3, Release 2.01, or the newer Release 2.2. All of the keystroke instructions will work exactly the same for either release. All of the screens displayed in the tutorial are as they would appear in Release 2.2; in some cases there will be slight differences in the appearance of Release 2.01 screens. The tutorials cover some features of Release 2.2 that are not available in Release 2.01. This is noted in the text, and you may skip over this material without a loss in continuity.

The tutorials will assume that you have access to 1-2-3 via one of three media: (1) the System Disk, a floppy disk that came when you purchased 1-2-3; (2) a subdirectory of a hard disk that contains copies of the 1-2-3 program files; or (3) a network menu system that allows downloading of 1-2-3 program files to your computer. The tutorials will also assume that you will store the worksheets you create on a formatted data disk (floppy) or a data subdirectory of the hard disk. You may also need an operating system disk (PC-DOS or MS-DOS) if you need to boot your computer when you start.

If needed, Appendix A contains a brief set of instructions for formatting a data disk, backing up and installing 1-2-3 for a two floppy disk system, and installing 1-2-3 for a hard disk system. Although these tasks are relatively straightforward, you might want to ask for help if you do not have much experience in performing them.

Entering 1-2-3 Commands

Throughout this book, a consistent notation will be used to identify keystrokes. When a key is to be pressed by itself, the key will appear by itself; for example,

Esc

If two keys are to be pressed in *combination*, the key symbols will be separated by the word *and*; for example,

Ctrl *and* →

Combinations are executed in three distinct steps. In this example, first hold down the Ctrl key. Next, press → once, as though you were typing a single character, and then release it. Finally, release Ctrl.

The majority of 1-2-3 functions are accessed by pressing a *sequence* of keystrokes (press the first, release it, then press the second, release it, and so on). 1-2-3 is a menu-driven software product; to perform a task, the user selects an item from a list of choices called a menu. The process begins by pressing the slash (/) key (located on the same key as the question mark). This causes a list of one-word menu items to be displayed horizontally across the top of the screen. One of these items is selected by pressing the first letter of the menu choice you desire. Depending on the letter selected, a new menu will appear, and another selection is made by pressing the first letter of the next menu choice. This process might continue for five or more levels before a task is complete. The sequential keystrokes required to select a series of menu items will be indicated by listing the keys to be pressed horizontally. The corresponding menu items selected will be spelled out below the keystrokes. For example, to exit 1-2-3, you will be asked to press

This indicates that the keys /, Q, and Y are to be pressed sequentially.

A Look Ahead

This book does not pretend to cover every 1-2-3 feature; the intent is to help you learn to use this powerful electronic spreadsheet program. This book is organized as a series of tutorials. In Chapter 2 you will learn how to create a spreadsheet, experiment with the spreadsheet, print a copy, and save the spreadsheet on disk. Chapter 3 introduces more sophisticated ways to format the spreadsheet. In subsequent chapters you will learn how to develop spreadsheets more efficiently, produce graphs, treat the spreadsheet as a database, and create macro programs. When you finish the tutorials, you will be able to use the 1-2-3 Reference Manual to learn additional features on your own.

Many tutorials assume that the reader will follow the instructions to the letter and that nothing will go wrong. That's not always true. Instructions can be misinterpreted. A user might decide to experiment. Hardware (or software) might fail. Throughout this book, you'll find a series of boxes labeled "What Can Go Wrong?" They anticipate common problems, explain what probably happened, and suggest how you might recover from the error condition.

You'll find quite a number of these boxes in Chapter 2 because when you first start using any new software package, you are likely to make errors. As your skill increases, errors will be less common, and those you do encounter will seem easier to correct; thus the number of "What Can Go Wrong?" boxes will decrease as you move from chapter to chapter.

Of course, not every error can be anticipated, and some problems (a disk failure, for example) require expert attention. If you can't find a solution to your problem, ask for help. If no help is available, you might try turning off the computer and starting over again.

Don't just read the chapter tutorials; you can't learn 1-2-3 (or any computer application for that matter) by simply reading about it. Sit down at a computer and follow along, step by step. Look at the 1-2-3 menus as you press the required keys to see what's happening. If you commit a reasonable amount of time, you'll be surprised at how quickly your confidence and skill develop.

Summary

You'll find a summary of new 1-2-3 features at the end of each chapter and a complete summary of all features introduced in Appendix B. No features were introduced in Chapter 1.

Self-Test

The answers to self-tests are in Appendix C.

1. In a spreadsheet to calculate student grades, the rows would probably represent _____ and the columns _____.
2. A computer's physical components are called _____.
3. The process of loading the operating system into memory is called _____.
4. _____ is volatile. Thus if data are to be kept for an extended period, they are normally saved to _____.
5. (Alt) *and* (Esc) means to press the two keys _____.
6. Menu options in 1-2-3 are selected by pressing one or more keys _____.

Exercises

1. Briefly discuss the advantages of electronic spreadsheets over manual spreadsheets.
2. Develop a manual spreadsheet for each of the following applications mentioned in the chapter:
   a. Budget
   b. Economic analysis
   c. Batting average calculation
3. "A computer's memory is volatile." What does that mean? Why is this property of memory important?
4. What is secondary storage? Why is secondary storage used?
5. Distinguish between data displayed on a screen, data stored in memory, and data stored on disk.

Creating, Saving, and Printing a Worksheet

This chapter introduces the 1-2-3 features and commands that allow you to:

- start 1-2-3
- create a worksheet
- move the cursor around the worksheet
- enter labels, numbers, and formulas
- select menu options
- save a worksheet
- make changes to a worksheet
- print a worksheet
- exit 1-2-3

Starting 1-2-3

This first tutorial will show you how to enter, save, and print a spreadsheet (hereafter called a "worksheet" to be consistent with the 1-2-3 Reference Manual). Don't just read through the tutorials. You will learn to use 1-2-3 much more quickly if you actually sit down at a computer and follow along, step by step.

Necessary Equipment

You will need an IBM PC, PS/2, or compatible computer equipped with a keyboard, a screen, a printer, and either two floppy disk drives or a hard disk. If you have a two-floppy-disk system, you'll also need the 1-2-3 System Disk, a formatted data disk, and a disk containing the disk operating system (DOS). If your computer has a hard disk, you probably won't need anything else. The 1-2-3 program files, the operating system, and your worksheet files should all be contained on the hard disk. Appendix A outlines the procedures for installing 1-2-3 on a floppy disk or hard disk and explains how to format a data disk.

If you are using the facilities of a microcomputer laboratory, your starting procedures will likely be different from those described in the following two sections. You will probably not need to "boot the operating system," and you may be asked to "load the 1-2-3 programs" from a network server. In this case, all you will probably need is a formatted data disk to store your worksheet files. Check with the manager of the laboratory to determine the proper starting procedures.

Booting the Operating System

Let's get started. If your system has two floppy disk drives, insert the DOS disk into drive A; if you are using a hard disk system, leave the floppy disk drive empty. Turn on the computer. If the computer is already running, press the key combination Ctrl *and* Alt *and* Del.

The computer will respond by loading the operating system into memory. Once DOS is in memory, you'll be asked to enter the date and the time. Respond to "Enter new date:" by typing the current date and then pressing ↵.

```
Current date is Tue  1-01-1980
Enter new date (mm-dd-yy): 2-1-90
Current time is 00:00:14.61
Enter new time: 10:30

The IBM Personal Computer DOS
Version 3.30 (C)Copyright International Business Machines Corp 1981, 1987
              (C)Copyright Microsoft Corp 1981, 1986

A>
```

```
The date:

mm-dd-yy
       └─── a two digit (90) or
            four digit (1990) year
     ─── the day, between 1 and 31
   ─── the month, between 1 and 12
```

```
The time:

hh:mm
    └─── minutes, between 0 and 59
  ─── hours, between 0 and 23
```

Figure 2.1 After you finish loading the operating system, your screen should look like this. The last line is an A> prompt (on a floppy disk system) or a C> prompt (on a hard disk system). The rules for typing the date and time are summarized below the screen.

Respond to "Enter new time:" by typing the current time and then pressing ↵. Use 24-hour military time; for example, 10:15 A.M. is 10:15, and 2:30 in the afternoon is 14:30. It is important to enter the date and time accurately because the operating system records them when it saves a worksheet.

After the date and time have been entered (Fig. 2.1), DOS will display an identifying message and a **prompt** (A> on a two-disk system, C> or C:\> on a hard disk system). The prompt is the operating system's way of asking you what to do next. Once you see it, you're ready to load the 1-2-3 program.

Keystroke Summary: Boot the operating system

Insert:	DOS disk in drive A
	(Skip this step on a hard disk system)
Turn on:	computer
	or
Press:	Ctrl *and* Alt *and* Del
Type:	*current date* (mm-dd-yy)
Press:	↵
Type:	*current time* (hh.mm)
Press:	↵

What Can Go Wrong?

1. "System not found", "Insert system disk", or a similar message appears on the screen. On an IBM PC, the screen reads "The IBM Personal Computer BASIC."

Cause: On a floppy disk system the operating system is not stored on the disk you placed in drive A. On a hard disk system you accidentally had a non-DOS disk in drive A.

Solution: On a floppy disk system, check to be sure you have the right disk in drive A; if you don't, change it. Otherwise, obtain another DOS disk and repeat the boot procedure. On a hard disk system, remove the disk from drive A and repeat the boot procedure.

2. A message suggests that the drive door may be open.

Cause: A disk cannot be read with the drive door open.

Solution: Close the drive door and repeat the boot procedure.

3. A message indicates that the date (or the time) is invalid.

Cause: You probably typed the date or time using an incorrect format.

Solution: Check the proper format for typing the date or the time (Fig. 2.1), and retype.

4. You know you typed the wrong date or time, but the computer accepted it.

Cause: You made a typing error, but the format was correct.

Solution: To correct the date, type the word DATE after the prompt and then press ⏎. To correct the time, type TIME and press ⏎. The operating system will let you try again.

Loading 1-2-3 on a Two-Floppy-Disk System

Skip this section if you are using a hard disk system. If you have correctly booted DOS, your screen should look like Fig. 2.1. The cursor should follow the A> prompt. Replace the DOS disk in drive A with the 1-2-3 System Disk. Insert the formatted data disk in drive B. Type

123

and then press

⏎

This loads the 1-2-3 program from the disk in drive A into memory and begins execution of the program. A 1-2-3 logo and some messages will appear briefly on the screen; then you will see an empty worksheet as illustrated in Fig. 2.2.

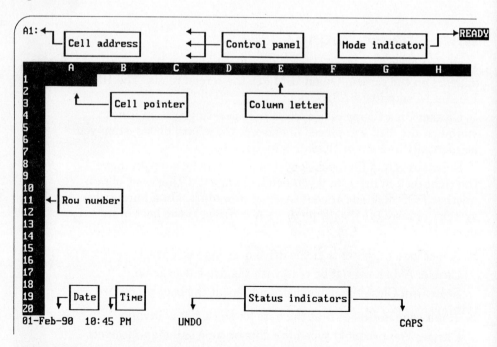

Figure 2.2 The 1-2-3 work screen simulates a worksheet of columns and rows. The cell pointer highlights the cell indicated by the cell address. Valuable information is displayed in the control panel and the status line.

14

Loading 1-2-3 on a Hard Disk System

Skip this section if you are using a two-floppy-disk system. If you have properly booted your hard disk system, the last line will look like Fig. 2.1 except that A> is replaced by C> (or C:\>) followed by the cursor. Type

CD \123

and then press

⏎

CD is a DOS command that changes the default directory of the hard disk. Following it is a backslash and then the name of a directory, 123, that stores all of your 1-2-3 program files.

After you press ⏎, the hard disk should activate, and a short time later, a new C> or C:\123> prompt should appear on the screen. Type

123

and press

⏎

This loads the 1-2-3 program from the 123 directory of the hard disk into memory and begins executing the program. A 1-2-3 logo and some messages will appear briefly on the screen; then you will see an empty worksheet as illustrated in Fig. 2.2.

Keystroke Summary: Load 1-2-3

Two-floppy-disk system:

Insert:	System Disk in drive A and data disk in drive B
Type:	**123**
Press:	⏎

Hard disk system:

Type:	**CD \123**
Press:	⏎
Type:	**123**
Press:	⏎

What Can Go Wrong?

1. Following the CD \123 command (on hard disk), a message indicates that the directory does not exist or could not be found.

Cause: The 1-2-3 program files are not on your hard disk or they are stored in a directory with a different name than 123.

Solution: If the 1-2-3 program files are not on your hard disk, follow the installation instructions given in Appendix A. Otherwise, ask the person who installed 1-2-3 on your hard disk for the name of the directory containing the 1-2-3 program files. Replace 123 in the command CD \123 with the directory name containing the program files.

2. After you type 123, a "File not found" message appears.

Cause: You might have misspelled the program name. The disk in drive A might not contain 1-2-3. On a hard disk system the program might not be stored on the disk.

Solution: First, be sure you typed the program name, 123, correctly by typing it again. If the same message reappears, make sure you are using the 1-2-3 system disk in drive A or that 1-2-3 is available in the 123 directory of your hard disk.

The 1-2-3 Work Screen

Study the empty work screen illustrated in Fig. 2.2. The center of the screen simulates a worksheet composed of rows and columns. The columns of the worksheet are labeled with letters, and the rows are labeled with numbers. An individual element of the worksheet where a column intersects a row is called a **cell**. A cell is designated by a column letter followed by a row number (for example, A1, B14, E4). The current cell is highlighted by the **cell pointer** and indicated by the **cell address** at the upper left corner of the screen.

The top three lines of the screen are called the **control panel**. Keep an eye on these lines as you follow the tutorial; they often provide useful information or instructions. For example, the cell address indicates the current position of the cell pointer. The **mode indicator** displays keywords such as READY, WAIT, or MENU. READY indicates that 1-2-3 is ready for you to enter information in the worksheet. WAIT indicates that 1-2-3 is performing computations and is not ready. MENU is displayed when 1-2-3 is accepting menu selections. At times, other information appears on lines 2 and 3 to give you feedback on what 1-2-3 is doing and to prompt you for input data.

The last line of the screen contains an optional date and time display and several status indicators. For example, CAPS, at the lower right side of the screen, is an indicator that the [Caps Lock] key is toggled on. Try pressing the [Caps Lock] key and notice how the status indicator for CAPS toggles on and off with each press. There is a similar indicator for the [Num Lock] key. The UNDO indicator tells you that you can press a certain key combination to cancel the last operation. This feature is not available in Release 2.01.

Creating a Worksheet

You are now ready to begin the tutorial. In this chapter you will create the example worksheet shown in Fig. 2.3. This worksheet represents a personal budget. A title appears in row 1, and a person's annual income appears in row 2. The worksheet is used to break the annual income figure into five budget categories: housing, food, transportation, clothing, and entertainment. The percentages of annual income allocated to each category are multiplied by the annual income to calculate the amount to be spent annually in each category. The monthly budgeted expenditure is computed by dividing the annual amount by 12. This personal budget worksheet will be used in several chapters to illustrate how worksheets are created and manipulated with 1-2-3.

As with manual worksheets, electronic worksheets are created by organizing the worksheet information into a set of rows and columns. This information is then entered into the worksheet one cell at a time. 1-2-3 classifies the data in a cell as a **label, number,** or **formula**. Worksheet titles, column headings, and row descriptions are examples of labels. Numeric constants (such as the annual income figure and the percentages for each budget category in Fig. 2.3) are called numbers. Numeric values that are calculated (such as the annual housing budget of 0.3 times 30,000) are created by entering formulas. In general, worksheets are created by positioning the cell pointer on a particular cell and entering a label, a number, or a formula into that cell position. You'll begin by learning to position the cell pointer.

Positioning the Cell Pointer

The cell pointer is positioned by using the cursor control keys; see Fig. 2.4 for a summary of the keys you'll be using. When you are beginning to create a

```
A12:                                                           READY

        A        B        C        D        E       F       G       H
1   BUDGET EXPENDITURE BY YEAR AND MONTH
2   ANNUAL INCOME        30000
3   ======================================================================
4   CATEGORY            PERCENTAGE        ANNUAL    MONTH
5   ======================================================================
6   HOUSING               0.3             9000       750
7   FOOD                  0.2             6000       500
8   TRANSPORTATION        0.1             3000       250
9   CLOTHING              0.1             3000       250
10  ENTERTAINMENT         0.3             9000       750
11  ======================================================================
12
```

Figure 2.3 This is the finished worksheet that you will be creating in the tutorial presented in this chapter.

Press	To Move the Cell Pointer
↑	one cell up
↓	one cell down
→	one cell to the right
←	one cell to the left
Home	to the upper left corner
PgDn	one screen down
PgUp	one screen up
Ctrl and →	one screen to the right
Ctrl and ←	one screen to the left
F5	to a particular cell address

Figure 2.4 Use these keys to position the cell pointer.

worksheet, the cell pointer is positioned at cell A1. Locate the cursor control keys on your keyboard.

Press → and the cell pointer moves one cell to the right, and the cell address in the upper left corner of the screen changes to B1 to indicate the current position of the cell pointer. Press ↓ and the cell pointer moves one cell down; press ← to move one cell to the left and ↑ to move one cell up. Each time you move the cell pointer, notice that the cell address changes to indicate the current position of the cell pointer.

Hold down → and the cell pointer moves rapidly to the right. (Release the key after several cells.) If you hold a key down, its action is repeated until you release the key.

Frequently, a worksheet contains more rows and/or columns than can be shown on the screen. To see additional columns, position the cell pointer on the right edge of the screen and press →. Repeat this several times, and the columns will scroll left across the screen. To see additional rows, position the cell pointer at the bottom of the screen and press ↓. Continue to press ↓ several more times and watch the rows scroll up the screen.

Look at Fig. 2.5 to see what is happening. The worksheet may be several hundred rows in length by several hundred columns in width, yet the screen shows only 8 columns and 20 rows of the worksheet at a time. When you position the cell pointer on the right edge and press →, the screen moves to the right one column to display an additional column of the worksheet. It appears to you that the columns have moved left across the screen. Likewise, when you position the cell pointer at the bottom of the screen and press ↓, the screen moves down one row to include a new row on the screen; the top

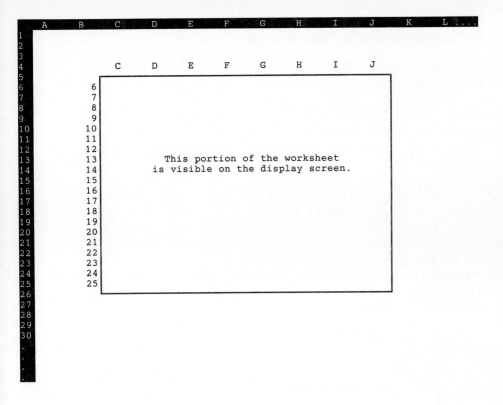

Figure 2.5 The display screen is capable of displaying only a portion of the worksheet at a time.

row scrolls off. Though most of the worksheets in the tutorial fit within the bounds of the display screen, most real applications require worksheets with more rows and columns than will fit on the display screen at one time. To return the cell pointer to the upper left corner of the worksheet, press (Home).

When working with large worksheets, it is often convenient to move the cell pointer an entire screen at a time rather than a single cell at a time. Horizontal movement requires a combination of keys. To move the cell pointer one screen to the right, press (Ctrl) *and* (→); to move the cell pointer one screen to the left, press (Ctrl) *and* (←). Begin by pressing (Ctrl) *and* (→). Notice that the cell pointer is now positioned eight columns to the right. Press (Ctrl) *and* (←), and the cell pointer is positioned eight columns to the left.

Vertical movement is accomplished with a single key. To move the cell pointer one screen (20 rows) down, press (PgDn); to move the cell pointer one screen up, press (PgUp). Go ahead and try it. When you are finished experimenting, press (Home) to return the cell pointer to cell A1.

Finally, the cell pointer may be moved directly to a particular cell by using the function key [F5]. To illustrate, press

[F5]

The prompt

```
Enter address to go to: A1
```

appears on line 2 of the control panel. At this point, you may type the cell address to which you wish to move the cell pointer. Suppose you want cell Q38. Type

Q38

and this value will replace A1. Press

[↵]

The cell pointer is moved directly to cell Q38.

Practice positioning the cell pointer using all the keys listed in Fig. 2.4. Before you go on, you should be able to move the cell pointer quickly to any cell on the worksheet using these keys.

Keystroke Summary: Move cell pointer to a particular cell

Press: [F5]

Type: *cell address*

Press: [↵]

What Can Go Wrong?

1. You accidentally pressed a key other than a cursor control key, causing characters to appear on the second line of the control panel.

Cause: 1-2-3 thinks you are entering a label, number, or formula into the current cell position.

Solution: Press [Esc]. The escape key cancels the current action you are taking.

2. You pressed a cursor control key on the numeric keypad, but the cursor did not move. A numeric value appears on the second line of the control panel.

Cause: The [Num Lock] key is toggled on so that the numeric key pad is in use rather than the cursor control keys.

Solution: Press [Esc] to cancel the current action. Then press [Num Lock] to switch from the numeric keypad to the cursor control keys.

Entering Labels and Numbers

This section begins the creation of the budget example by entering labels and numbers into the appropriate cells. Recall that descriptive information such as titles, column headings, and row labels is entered as labels and numeric constants are entered as numbers. Both labels and numbers are used to represent information that does not change. They are entered by positioning the cell pointer over the desired cell and typing the label or number to be placed in that cell. On the other hand, formulas that represent calculated numeric values do change; they are discussed in the next section.

Begin by entering the title of the worksheet (a label) into cell A1. Position the cell pointer to cell A1 (press Home).

Type the first entry (Fig. 2.6):

BUDGET EXPENDITURE BY YEAR AND MONTH

Hold down ⊕ and press each character in turn. Better yet, use the Caps Lock key. The Caps Lock key works like a toggle switch. Press Caps Lock once, and the alphabetic keys generate capital letters. Press it again, and the keyboard returns to lowercase letters. Note that only the alphabetic keys are affected; for example, if you press a 1, you will enter the digit 1 no matter how the Caps Lock key is set. The state of the Caps Lock key is indicated by a status indicator on line 25 of the screen.

As soon as you begin typing this entry, the mode indicator switches from READY to LABEL, indicating that a label is being prepared for entry into the current cell. A label is simply a string of characters that will appear exactly as entered on the worksheet. As each character is typed, it will appear on line 2 of the control panel. If you make any typing errors, press ← (*not* ←) to erase the previous character; then retype it. Make sure your screen looks like Fig. 2.6 before continuing. If it doesn't, press Esc and try again.

Now press

↵

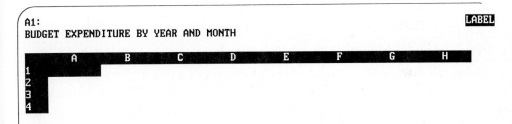

Figure 2.6 For entering a label, the mode indicator changes from READY to LABEL. The information entered appears on line 2 of the control panel until the ↵ key is pressed.

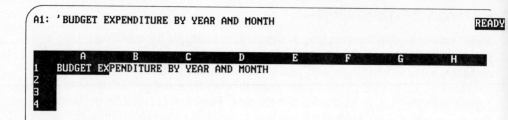

A1: 'BUDGET EXPENDITURE BY YEAR AND MONTH   READY

Figure 2.7 When the ⏎ key is pressed, the label is moved to the worksheet and displayed on line 1 of the control panel. Whenever the cell pointer is pointing to a given cell, its contents will be displayed on line 1. Notice also the label-prefix character preceding the label definition.

This moves the label from the second line of the control panel to the highlighted position on the worksheet as illustrated in Fig. 2.7. All cell entries, labels, numbers, and formulas are initially displayed on line 2 of the control panel and moved onto the worksheet when you press ⏎ or any of the cell pointer positioning keys listed in Fig. 2.4. Once the ⏎ key is pressed, the label is moved to the worksheet, line 2 of the control panel is cleared, and the mode indicator is reset to READY.

Notice that line 1 of the control panel displays the current contents of the highlighted cell. If the cell pointer is moved, the cell address and the cell contents on line 1 will change to indicate the address and contents of the highlighted cell.

The control panel entry in cell A1 is preceded by an apostrophe (') character. This is called a **label-prefix character**. One of these characters (see Fig. 2.8 for a list of label-prefix characters) precedes each label entry and indicates how the label is to be positioned in the cell. The ' character indicates that the label in this cell is to be aligned at the left edge of the cell. Other characters are used to position a label in the center of the cell (^), to align the label with the right edge of the cell ("), and to repeat the label across the width of the cell (\). The label-prefix character may be typed as the label is

Prefix Character	Label Position
'	aligns label with left edge of cell
"	aligns label with right edge of cell
^	centers label between left and right edges of cell
\	repeats label across width of cell

Figure 2.8 Use these label-prefix characters to position labels in the worksheet cell.

22

entered, or, as in this case, the default label-prefix will be entered automatically by 1-2-3.

Finally, notice that the label entry in cell A1 extends into cells B1, C1, and D1. Labels that are too long to fit in a single column are permitted to extend over columns to the right *provided that the following cells are empty*. If an entry is made in one of the following cells, the label is truncated to fit in the space available. However, the entire label is stored so that if the following cells are later empty, the entire label may be displayed again.

Now continue the example by positioning the cell pointer to cell A2 and typing

'ANNUAL INCOME

Press ⏎. This time, you are typing the label-prefix character ' as part of the label.

Now you'll see the effect of entering a number in the worksheet. Enter the annual income figure by positioning the cell pointer to cell C2 (Fig. 2.9) and typing

30000

As soon as you begin typing, the mode indicator changes to VALUE. This indicates that the current cell will contain numeric information, either the direct entry of a number, as in this case, or the implied entry of a number via a formula, as described in the next section. 1-2-3 classifies both numbers and formulas as values.

As before, the cell entry is initially displayed on line 2 of the control panel. ⬅ may be used to erase and correct the previously typed character, and (Esc) may be used to abandon the cell entry and start over again.

Press

⏎

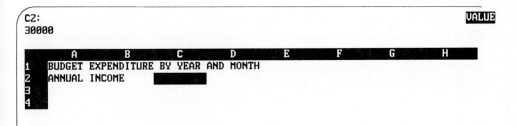

Figure 2.9 When a number is entered, the mode indicator changes from READY to VALUE. The number entered appears on line 2 of the control panel until the ⏎ key is pressed, as with labels.

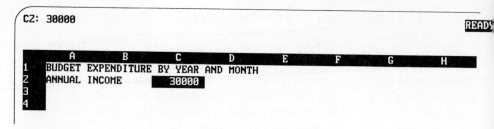

	A	B	C	D	E	F	G	H
1	BUDGET EXPENDITURE BY YEAR AND MONTH							
2	ANNUAL INCOME		30000					
3								
4								

Figure 2.10 When the ↵ key is pressed, the number is moved to the worksheet and displayed on line 1 of the control panel. Numbers do not use label-prefix characters; they are aligned with the right edge of the cell.

The number 30000 is entered in worksheet cell C2 and displayed on line 1 of the control panel (Fig. 2.10). The mode indicator returns to READY mode. There is no label-prefix character because numeric information is always aligned with the right edge of the cell. (In the next chapter you will learn how to control the position of the decimal point and other format features of numbers.)

You may be curious to know how 1-2-3 determines whether the entry you are making in a cell is a label or a value. It all depends on the first key pressed. The entry will be considered a value if it begins with any of the following characters: 0 1 2 3 4 5 6 7 8 9 . + − $ (@ #. Otherwise, it will be considered a label.

This raises the question of how you create a label composed of numbers. For example, suppose you wish to create a label called 123. You can enter 123 as a label by preceding the entry of 123 with a label-prefix character such as ^ (located on number key 6). Entering ^123 will cause the 1-2-3 program to treat the digits 123 as a label that is centered in the cell.

Since pressing any key begins the creation of a label or value in the highlighted cell, accidentally pressing a key will also begin this process. To stop a cell entry process that is begun accidentally, press Esc.

Return to the example in Fig. 2.3. Notice that rows 3, 5, and 11 contain a series of equal signs (=) to highlight the column headings and boundaries of the table. Creating table boundary characters can be accomplished by creating a label composed of an appropriate number of equal signs (or other characters) in each cell position. However, it is more convenient and flexible to use the repeating label-prefix character as illustrated in Fig. 2.11. Try it. Position the cell pointer to cell A3 and type

    \=

Press

    ↵

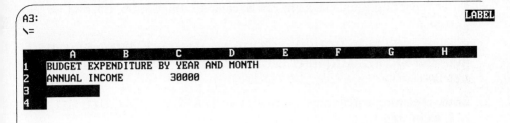

Figure 2.11 The backslash (\) character is a label-prefix character designed to repeat the label entered across the entire width of the cell. Entering \= will produce a cell full of equals signs for a worksheet divider.

Cell A3 will be filled with equals signs. The backslash (\) is a label-prefix character to indicate that the equals sign (or other symbol you may choose) is to be repeated across the entire cell width.

Practice your skills at entering labels and numbers, creating a copy of the example up to the point illustrated in Fig. 2.12. Use the following steps:

1. Complete row 3 by entering repeating equals signs in cells B3, C3, D3, E3, and F3 as you did in cell A3.

2. Enter the column headings CATEGORY, PERCENTAGE, ANNUAL, and MONTHLY as labels in cells A4, C4, E4, and F4 in the same way you did the labels in A1 and A2.

```
E6:                                                              READY

      A         B         C         D         E         F         G         H
1  BUDGET EXPENDITURE BY YEAR AND MONTH
2  ANNUAL INCOME          30000
3  =====================================================================
4  CATEGORY            PERCENTAGE           ANNUAL    MONTHLY
5  =====================================================================
6  HOUSING                 0.3        ▓▓▓▓▓▓▓▓▓▓
7  FOOD                    0.2
8  TRANSPORTATION          0.1
9  CLOTHING                0.1
10 ENTERTAINMENT           0.3
11 =====================================================================
12
```

Figure 2.12 The example worksheet will look like this when all of the labels and numbers have been entered.

3. Enter repeating equals signs in row 5, cells A5, B5, C5, D5, E5, and F5, as in step 1.

4. Enter the row labels HOUSING, FOOD, TRANSPORTATION, CLOTH-ING, and ENTERTAINMENT in cells A6, A7, A8, A9, and A10, as in step 2.

5. Enter repeating equals signs in row 11, cells A11, B11, C11, D11, E11, and F11, as in step 1.

6. Enter the percentages to be used for each budget category as numbers in cells C6, C7, C8, C9, and C10 in the same way you entered the annual income in cell C2.

In general, you may enter information into the cells in any order. Numbers may begin with a zero or a decimal point. The process of entering equals signs (the boundary character in the example) in 18 cells may seem a little tedious, but you will learn some shortcuts for doing this in Chapter 4. The remaining entries in the example require you to enter formulas that are discussed in the next section.

What Can Go Wrong?

1. You made a mistake entering a label or number in a cell and pressed a cursor control key to go back and correct your mistake. The incorrect information is now entered in your worksheet.

Cause: A label or number is entered in the worksheet by pressing ⏎ as described above *or* by moving the cell pointer to another cell using the cursor movement keys. Thus when you pressed the cursor movement key to correct your cell entry, the cell pointer was moved, and the entry in the cell was completed.

Solution: Reposition the cell pointer on the incorrect cell. Type in the correct label or number and press ⏎. This entry will then replace the incorrect entry. Later in this chapter you will learn a better method of correcting or editing the contents of a cell. Until then, use ⬅ to correct typing mistakes.

2. You entered a label or number in the wrong cell position.

Cause: The cell pointer was not positioned over the correct cell when you typed the label or number.

Solution: Position the cell pointer over the contents of the incorrect cell location. Erase the contents of the cell using the following sequence of keystrokes. You are using the 1-2-3 menus, which are explained later in this chapter.

Press: / R E
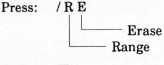
                        └──── Erase
                 └──── Range

Press: ⏎

3. You typed the backslash label-prefix character, and the mode indicator changed to MENU rather than LABEL.

Cause: Instead of pressing the backslash key (\) as intended, you pressed the slash (/) key. The slash (/) key activates the menu system.

Solution: Press Esc to exit the menu system and try again using the backslash key (\).

Undoing the Last Operation

Beginning with Release 2.2, Lotus 1-2-3 provides an UNDO feature to cancel the last cell entry or the results of the last operation. UNDO is a convenient way to correct mistakes. To illustrate, move the cell pointer to cell A1 and type the label

    THIS IS A MISTAKE

Then press ⏎ to enter the erroneous label in cell A1 (Fig. 2.13).

To correct the error, press

    Alt *and* F4

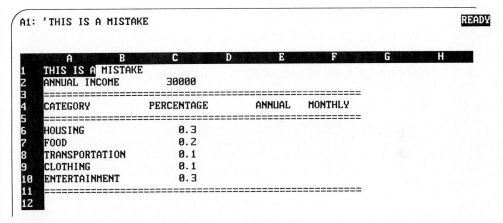

Figure 2.13 An erroneous label is entered in cell A1.

in combination, and the last operation is canceled. The worksheet will once again resemble Fig. 2.12.

Press ⌐Alt⌐ *and* ⌐F4⌐ again. Note that the erroneous label reappears. This key combination acts as a toggle switch, allowing you to do and undo the last operation as many times as you wish. Press ⌐Alt⌐ *and* ⌐F4⌐ one more time to restore the worksheet to the correct title. As you continue the tutorial, use this feature as necessary to cancel the most recent cell entry or the most recent menu operation.

Entering Formulas

Now that you have learned how to enter labels and numbers into a worksheet, you might be thinking that this seems like a lot of work without much advantage. You are right! The real power of electronic spreadsheet programs is obtained by using formulas. Formulas are used to define cell values that are calculated from other numeric values in a worksheet. Formulas are used to compute row totals and column totals or, more generally, to perform any calculation involving the addition, subtraction, multiplication, or division of values contained in worksheet cells. In the budget example, the annual and monthly amounts budgeted in each category can be calculated via formulas from values in other cells of the worksheet. Let's see how a formula is defined.

Position the cell pointer over cell E6. In this cell you wish to display the annual amount available for housing. This number is 0.3 of the 30,000 dollar annual income, which equals 9000 dollars. You could enter 9000 as a number in this cell, but if you later wished to change the annual income or the percentage allowance for housing, you would also have to change the contents of this cell.

A better way to express the contents of this cell is as a formula. A formula is an instruction to 1-2-3 to calculate the contents of a cell using an equation that may include references to values in other cell positions. Type the formula

    +C2*C6

as illustrated in Fig. 2.14. This formula is an instruction to calculate the value of the current cell by multiplying the value in cell C2 by the value in cell C6. The initial plus sign is necessary to inform 1-2-3 that the entry you are working with is a numeric value. (If you typed C2*C6, this entry would be treated as a label.) The asterisk is an operator used to indicate that a multiplication operation is to take place. (Other common operators are + for addition, – for subtraction, and / for division.) Complete the cell entry by pressing

    ⏎

The value 9000 appears on the worksheet in cell E6. The contents of cell E6 on line 1 of the control panel are recorded as a formula rather than a number.

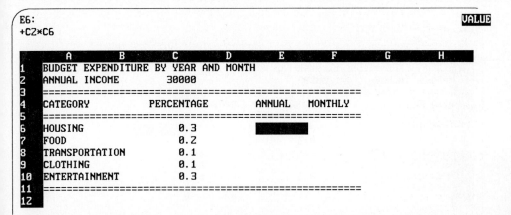

Figure 2.14 The amount in cell E6 is computed by a formula that multiplies the contents of cell C2 times the contents of cell C6. The formula is preceded by a plus sign to make sure 1-2-3 will not treat this entry as a label. The result will be a number, and so the mode indicator is set to VALUE.

This way, if the value of cell C2 or C6 changes, the value of cell E6 will change automatically.

Now consider cell E7. Its value may be calculated by a similar formula that multiplies the annual income (30000 in cell C2) by the food percentage (0.2 in cell C7). An appropriate formula is +C2*C7. Position the cell pointer over cell E7 and type

    +C2*C7

Press ⏎, and the value 6000 will appear in cell E7. Practice by entering similar formulas in cells E8, E9, and E10 to calculate the annual budget amount for each of the remaining categories (+C2*C8, +C2*C9, and +C2*C10, respectively).

The monthly allocation for each budget category is also an appropriate use of a formula because the allocation is related to other items on the worksheet. Specifically, the monthly budget allocation for housing can be calculated by dividing the annual income (cell C2) by 12 and multiplying the result by 0.3 (the value in cell C6). In this case an appropriate formula is +(C2/12)*C6. Parentheses are used to make sure that the division takes place before the multiplication.

Alternatively, the monthly budget allocation for housing can be calculated by dividing the annual budget allocation for housing (cell E6) by 12. This is a simpler approach. Position the cell pointer to cell F6. Type the formula

    +E6/12

as illustrated Fig. 2.15. In a formula you can refer to another cell whose value is the result of a formula because 1-2-3 automatically makes sure that all

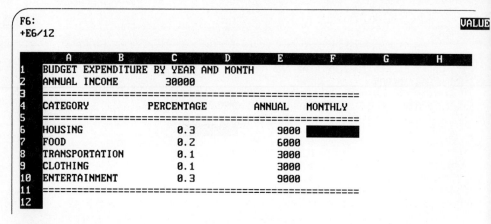

	A	B	C	D	E	F	G	H
1	BUDGET EXPENDITURE BY YEAR AND MONTH							
2	ANNUAL INCOME		30000					
3	===							
4	CATEGORY		PERCENTAGE		ANNUAL	MONTHLY		
5	===							
6	HOUSING		0.3		9000			
7	FOOD		0.2		6000			
8	TRANSPORTATION		0.1		3000			
9	CLOTHING		0.1		3000			
10	ENTERTAINMENT		0.3		9000			
11	===							
12								

Figure 2.15 The content of cell F6 is computed by a formula that divides the values in cell E6 by 12. 1-2-3 automatically makes sure that the formula for cell E6 is computed before the formula for cell F6.

formulas are calculated in the proper order. That is, the formula in E6 will be calculated before the formula in F6. Press

⏎

and the value 750 appears on the worksheet in cell F6.

The remaining monthly budget allocations may be calculated by using formulas that divide the annual budget allocations by 12. Complete the sample worksheet by entering similar formulas in cells F7, F8, F9, and F10 (+E7/12, +E8/12, +E9/12, and +E10/12, respectively).

What Can Go Wrong?

1. The formula that you entered appeared in the worksheet cell rather than the computed value.

Cause: The formula was treated as a label rather than a formula.

Solution: Position the cell pointer on the problem worksheet cell. Retype the formula beginning with a + and press ⏎. The initial plus sign is a signal that this cell contains a value. If the formula starts with a cell address, such as C2, the initial letter C signals 1-2-3 that this cell contains a label.

1-2-3 Menus

Congratulations, you have now completed your first worksheet. You know how to position the cell pointer and enter labels, numbers, and formulas into worksheet cells. Please do not stop the tutorial here. At this point the worksheet is stored in the computer's memory and will be lost when you turn the machine off. You need to save the worksheet from memory to disk. To do this, you need to learn about the 1-2-3 **menu** system.

Press

/

This gives you access to the 1-2-3 menu system. A menu, as the name suggests, provides a list of items to choose from. You will be called upon to select one of these items. Often, when you select one item, another menu or list of items is provided for you to choose from. The process of selecting menu items might continue for several levels before a task is complete.

Fig. 2.16 displays the first level of menu options obtained by pressing the / key. The mode indicator is changed to MENU, and a series of one-word menu options is displayed horizontally across the second line of the control panel. A brief description of each of the main menu options is given in Fig. 2.17.

```
A12:                                                             MENU
Worksheet  Range  Copy  Move  File  Print  Graph  Data  System  Add-In  Quit
Global  Insert  Delete  Column  Erase  Titles  Window  Status  Page  Learn
         A          B          C          D       E       F       G       H
1  BUDGET EXPENDITURE BY YEAR AND MONTH
2  ANNUAL INCOME          30000
3  ==================================================================
4  CATEGORY              PERCENTAGE          ANNUAL   MONTHLY
5  ==================================================================
6  HOUSING                  0.3              9000       750
7  FOOD                     0.2              6000       500
8  TRANSPORTATION           0.1              3000       250
9  CLOTHING                 0.1              3000       250
10 ENTERTAINMENT            0.3              9000       750
11 ==================================================================
12
```

Figure 2.16 Line 2 of the control panel displays a list of one-word menu items. These are the main menu choices. Line 3 displays the second-level list of menu items available if the highlighted option (Worksheet) is selected. The mode indicator is set to MENU.

Menu Choice	Provides Options for
Worksheet	modifying the entire worksheet
Range	modifying a portion of the worksheet
Copy	copying the contents of a specific set of worksheet cells to another location
Move	moving the contents of a specific set of worksheet cells to another location
File	saving or retrieving worksheets to or from disk storage
Print	printing a worksheet or portion of a worksheet on your printer
Graph	creating graphs using the data obtained from the worksheet
Data	sorting and searching the data in your worksheet
System	temporarily returning to the operating system, leaving 1-2-3 and your worksheet in memory
Add-In	for using add-in programs created by Lotus and other software developers
Quit	returning to the operating system and removing 1-2-3 and your worksheet from memory

Figure 2.17 The main menu in 1-2-3 is organized above.

Line 3 of the control panel either describes the function performed by the highlighted menu item or lists the menu items at the next level below the highlighted menu item. In Fig. 2.16, Worksheet is highlighted, and the list of menu items at the next level under Worksheet is displayed on line 3. If the Worksheet option is selected, the list on the third line would move up to the second line and become available for selection.

When in MENU selection mode, the ⊟ and ⊟ keys no longer move the cell pointer but allow you to highlight different menu items. Press ⊟. This highlights the Range option and displays on line 3 of the control panel the menu items at the next level under Range. Press ⊟ again and review the description under the Copy option. Move the cursor to highlight each menu option. Read line 3 for each menu option so that you begin to get familiar with the options under each main menu choice.

There are two ways to select a menu option. One is to use the ⊟ and ⊟ keys to highlight the desired option and then press ⊒ to perform the selection. To illustrate, use

⊟

```
A12:                                                                    MENU
Worksheet  Range  Copy  Move  [File]  Print  Graph  Data  System  Add-In  Quit
Retrieve  Save  Combine  Xtract  Erase  List  Import  Directory  Admin
         A          B          C          D          E       F       G        H
1    BUDGET EXPENDITURE BY YEAR AND MONTH
2    ANNUAL INCOME            30000
3    ===================================================================
4    CATEGORY              PERCENTAGE         ANNUAL    MONTHLY
5    ===================================================================
6    HOUSING                  0.3             9000       750
7    FOOD                     0.2             6000       500
8    TRANSPORTATION           0.1             3000       250
9    CLOTHING                 0.1             3000       250
10   ENTERTAINMENT            0.3             9000       750
11   ===================================================================
12
```

Figure 2.18 In this case, File is highlighted, so line 3 displays the second-level list of menu items if File is selected. These include retrieving files, saving files, combining files, and so forth.

to highlight the File menu option (Fig. 2.18). Notice that the menu choices under the File option are displayed on line 3 of the control panel. Press ⏎ to select the File option. The menu choices under the File option are now displayed on line 2 of the control panel. Use → to highlight the Directory menu option (Fig. 2.19). Line 3 indicates that this option is used to "Display and/or change the current directory". Press ⏎, and line 2 will prompt you to enter the name of the directory where worksheet files are to be stored (Fig. 2.20).

```
A12:                                                                    MENU
Retrieve  Save  Combine  Xtract  Erase  List  Import  [Directory]  Admin
Display and/or change the current directory
         A          B          C          D          E       F       G        H
1    BUDGET EXPENDITURE BY YEAR AND MONTH
2    ANNUAL INCOME            30000
3    ===================================================================
4    CATEGORY              PERCENTAGE         ANNUAL    MONTHLY
5    ===================================================================
6    HOUSING                  0.3             9000       750
7    FOOD                     0.2             6000       500
8    TRANSPORTATION           0.1             3000       250
9    CLOTHING                 0.1             3000       250
10   ENTERTAINMENT            0.3             9000       750
11   ===================================================================
12
```

Figure 2.19 Menu option File has been selected. The second-level list of menu items is moved from line 3 to line 2 of the control panel. The second-level option Directory is highlighted, and line 3 describes the function of this menu item.

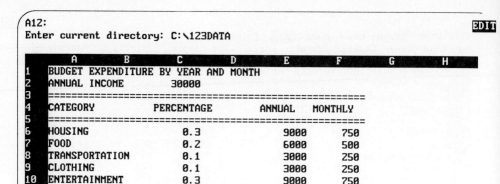

```
A12:                                                                   EDIT
Enter current directory: C:\123DATA

        A        B        C        D        E        F        G        H
1  BUDGET EXPENDITURE BY YEAR AND MONTH
2  ANNUAL INCOME          30000
3  ===========================================================
4  CATEGORY         PERCENTAGE      ANNUAL   MONTHLY
5  ===========================================================
6  HOUSING              0.3          9000      750
7  FOOD                 0.2          6000      500
8  TRANSPORTATION       0.1          3000      250
9  CLOTHING             0.1          3000      250
10 ENTERTAINMENT        0.3          9000      750
11 ===========================================================
12
```

Figure 2.20 Menu option Directory has been selected. You are being prompted either to accept the current directory by pressing ⏎ or to type the name of the directory in which you would like to store files. The mode indicator has changed to EDIT, since you are to type a response. Line 3 of the control panel is blank, since there are no further menu choices.

You may either type in a new directory name or press ⏎ to accept the directory name given. Press ⏎ to accept the directory name given and to return to READY mode. If you have any difficulty following these steps, press [Esc] until you return to READY mode and try again.

An alternative procedure for selecting menu options is to press the key corresponding to the first letter of the menu choice. Repeat the menu selections made above using this procedure. Make sure you are in READY mode and press

/

to activate the menu system and to display the main menu choices on line 2 of the control panel (Fig. 2.16). Press

F
└── File

to select the File menu option and display the File menu choices on line 2 of the control panel (Fig. 2.19). Press

D
└── Directory

to select the Directory menu option (Fig. 2.20). Press ⏎ to accept the directory name given and return to READY mode.

You may use either procedure to select menu choices in the tutorials. The first method (highlighting the menu choice and pressing ⏎) is slower but gives you the opportunity to look at the other menu options and read about them on line 3 of the control panel. It's also a useful method for exploring the menu system and learning new menu features. You are encouraged to use this method, especially during the early tutorials.

The second method (pressing the first letter of a menu choice) requires fewer keystrokes to select an option and thus is faster. Experienced 1-2-3 users tend to use this method because they are already familiar with the menu system. Use this method after you become more experienced.

In the tutorials you will be directed to select menu options using the second method. For the example illustrated above, the tutorial would instruct you to press

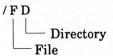

This is a convenient form for expository purposes and for reference purposes. However, when you encounter these instructions, please feel free to select the menu choices by highlighting the desired menu choices and pressing ⏎, especially until you become comfortable with the menu system.

Take some time now to explore some of the menu options (except Quit). Use ⏵ or ⏴ to highlight various menu choices and read the descriptions on line 3 of the control panel.

Press ⏎ to select some options and study the next set of menu choices. Work your way down through several levels of menus as desired. If you get confused, you can work your way back up through the menu levels by pressing

[Esc]

Each time [Esc] is pressed, you move up one menu level until you are out of the menu system completely and in READY mode. You can reenter the menu system by pressing the / key. Practice moving around in the menu system.

Keystroke Summary: Select menu option

Method 1:

    Press: /

    Press: ⏵ or ⏴ to highlight menu option choice

    Press: ⏎

Method 2:

    Press: /

    Press: first letter of menu option

Saving a Worksheet

You are now ready to copy the worksheet you created from the computer's memory to a disk file. This is accomplished by accessing the menu system and choosing the File option. The secondary menu under File has an option called Save, which is used to save a worksheet in a disk file. Press

```
/ F S
    |
    |——— Save
    |——— File
```

Remember that you can select these menu options by highlighting the desired choices and pressing ⏎. A message will appear on line 2 of the control panel:

```
Enter name of file to save: C:\123DATA\*.wk1
```

The cursor follows the message. 1-2-3 is telling you that the worksheet will be stored on the hard disk (drive C), in the directory 123DATA, with any file name that you specify (*), and with the extension WK1. If you are using a floppy disk system, the message will be slightly different:

```
Enter name of file to save: B:\*.wk1
```

This message indicates that the worksheet will be stored on a floppy disk (drive B), in the main or root directory, with any file name that you specify (*), and with the extension WK1.

It is possible to store many different worksheets (more generally, **files**) on a single disk. To distinguish among the worksheets or files, each must be assigned a unique name. It is your responsibility to name your files. A **file name** consists of one to eight characters. Although some punctuation marks are legal, others aren't, so restrict your name to combinations of letters and digits. Type either uppercase or lowercase letters. Following the file name, you can (optionally) type a period and add a one- to three-character **extension**. If you choose not to give an extension, then 1-2-3 will automatically add the extension WK1. Normally, you will choose a file name that suggests the worksheet contents and omit the extension. BUDGET might be a good choice. Type

BUDGET

Your screen will look like Fig. 2.21. Press

⏎

The mode indicator will switch briefly to WAIT while the worksheet is copied to a disk file and then will return to READY mode. Your worksheet is now stored on a floppy disk or a hard disk under the file name BUDGET.WK1. This is a convenient place to stop the tutorial if necessary.

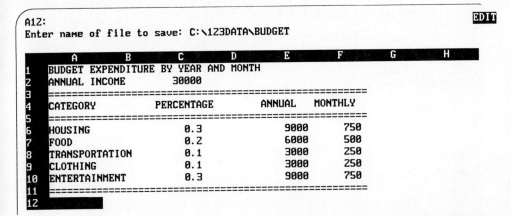

```
A12:                                                              EDIT
Enter name of file to save: C:\123DATA\BUDGET

        A       B       C       D       E       F       G       H
1  BUDGET EXPENDITURE BY YEAR AND MONTH
2  ANNUAL INCOME          30000
3  ==================================================================
4  CATEGORY           PERCENTAGE          ANNUAL   MONTHLY
5  ==================================================================
6  HOUSING                0.3              9000      750
7  FOOD                   0.2              6000      500
8  TRANSPORTATION         0.1              3000      250
9  CLOTHING               0.1              3000      250
10 ENTERTAINMENT          0.3              9000      750
11 ==================================================================
12
```

Figure 2.21 After choosing the menu options to save a file, you are prompted to enter the name to be given to your worksheet file. Type BUDGET, and the screen will appear as above. The file will be named BUDGET.WK1 and will be stored in the directory 123DATA of the C drive.

Keystroke Summary: Save a worksheet

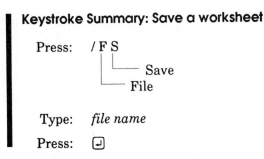

Press: / F S
            Save
            File

Type: *file name*

Press: ↵

What Can Go Wrong?

1. The drive letter or directory name following the message "Enter name of file to save" is incorrect. For example, A:\ is incorrect on a floppy disk system, since your data disk is in drive B. On a hard disk system you may see C:\dirname*.wk1 where dirname is not the name of the directory you wish to use to store your worksheet.

Cause: When 1-2-3 was initially set up, a certain drive letter and directory (the default directory) was established as the place where worksheet files are to be stored. You wish to store your files in a different location.

Solution: Change the default directory as follows:

Press: [Esc] until you return to READY mode

Press: / F D
```
        |
        |——— Directory
        |——— File
```

Type: **B:** for a floppy drive system

or

C:\dirname for a hard drive system

Press: [↵]

2. When the message "Enter name of file to save" appears on line 2 of the control panel, line 3 contains a list of file names and directory names with the first one highlighted.

Cause: There is really nothing wrong with this. 1-2-3 is providing you with a list of existing worksheet files and directory names (those names ending with a \ character). This allows you to select an existing file name or directory by pressing [→] or [←] until your choice is highlighted. Then press [↵].

Solution: No solution is required. Simply type in the file name and ignore the choices provided.

3. When you type the file name and press [↵], another menu appears, giving you the options Cancel, Replace, and Backup.

Cause: There is already a file on the disk with the name you chose.

Solution: Press C to choose the Cancel option. This will return you to READY mode and nothing will have been saved. Save the worksheet again, but choose a different file name.

Modifying a Worksheet

One of the most beneficial aspects of working with spreadsheets electronically is the ability to easily make modifications. You might wish to change the labels, numbers, formulas, layout, spacing, or formatting. You might also wish to add, delete, or relocate certain rows or columns, or you might wish to recalculate the formulas in the worksheet using different numeric values. You will now see how to **edit** the contents of a cell, using the budget worksheet example. You have already learned that you can change a label, number, or formula in a cell by retyping it, but in this section, you'll learn to change the contents of a cell by modifying (or editing) the previous contents. If the cell content contains only a few keystrokes, it is usually easier to retype, but if the cell contains many keystrokes and you only wish to make a small change, it is easier to edit.

'MONTHLY

	A	B	C	D	E	F	G	H
1	BUDGET EXPENDITURE BY YEAR AND MONTH							
2	ANNUAL INCOME		30000					
3	==
4	CATEGORY		PERCENTAGE		ANNUAL	MONTHLY		
5	==
6	HOUSING		0.3		9000	750		
7	FOOD		0.2		6000	500		
8	TRANSPORTATION		0.1		3000	250		
9	CLOTHING		0.1		3000	250		
10	ENTERTAINMENT		0.3		9000	750		
11	==
12								

Figure 2.22 Highlighting cell F4 and pressing F2 copies the contents of this cell onto line 2 of the control panel and allows you to modify or edit the contents of this cell. The mode indicator changes to EDIT.

To illustrate editing, suppose you wish to modify the column label MONTHLY so that it reads MONTH and is centered in the cell. To edit the contents of this cell, you need to change the label-prefix character from ' to ^ and to delete the last two letters, LY, from the label MONTHLY.

Begin by positioning the cell pointer to F4, which contains the label MONTHLY. Function key F2 is used to edit a cell. Press

F2

and you will obtain the screen shown in Fig. 2.22. You are in EDIT mode, and the contents of this cell have been copied to line 2 of the control panel for editing. The edit cursor is initially positioned at the end of the line. Once in EDIT mode, you may use the keys listed in Fig. 2.23 to perform the editing functions indicated.

Press	To Do the Following
→	move the edit cursor one position right
←	move the edit cursor one position left
Home	move the edit cursor to beginning of line
End	move the edit cursor to end of line
Del	delete the character at the edit cursor
Ins	insert or replace characters beginning at the edit cursor
↵	complete the entry and return to READY

Figure 2.23 Use these keys to edit the contents of a cell.

Creating, Saving, and Printing a Worksheet   **39**
Modifying a Worksheet

```
       A       B       C       D       E       F       G       H
1  BUDGET EXPENDITURE BY YEAR AND MONTH
2  ANNUAL INCOME        30000
3  =================================================================
4  CATEGORY         PERCENTAGE        ANNUAL    MONTH
5  =================================================================
6  HOUSING              0.3            9000      750
7  FOOD                 0.2            6000      500
8  TRANSPORTATION       0.1            3000      250
9  CLOTHING             0.1            3000      250
10 ENTERTAINMENT        0.3            9000      750
11 =================================================================
12
```

Figure 2.24 The label MONTHLY has been edited to MONTH and is centered in the cell rather than aligned with the left edge of the cell.

To change the label-prefix character from ' to ^, first press Home. Notice that the edit cursor is positioned under the ' character at the beginning of the line. Press Del and the character ' is deleted. Press ⇧ *and* ^ (key 6 above the alphabetic keys), and the ^ character is inserted in the first character position of the cell.

Delete the LY as follows. Use → to position the edit cursor under the L. Press Del twice, and both the L and Y will be deleted. Finally, press ⏎ to complete the editing of this entry and return to READY mode.

Your worksheet should now contain the label MONTH centered in cell position F4 (Fig. 2.24). For practice, edit another label such as the report heading in cell A1. Position the cell pointer on A1 and press F2. Try all the keys in Fig. 2.23 so that you're sure what they do. If you want to leave EDIT mode without saving the changes, press

Esc

to return to READY mode. You may have noticed by now that in 1-2-3 the Esc key allows you to return to a previous state without taking any action, while ⏎ is generally used to complete an action.

Next, edit a numeric value. Suppose you wish to change the annual income figure from 30000 to 45000. Return to READY mode and position the cell pointer at C2, the cell containing the numeric value 30000. Press F2 to enter EDIT mode. Change this numeric value to 45000 by pressing Home to position the edit cursor at the beginning of the line. Press Ins to change from insert to replacement mode, and type 45.

Now press ⏎ and watch the worksheet closely. Amazing! You changed one number, and all of the formulas based on annual income were automatically recalculated (Fig. 2.25). *The ability to change a number and have the work-*

40

```
        A       B       C       D       E       F       G       H
1  BUDGET EXPENDITURE BY YEAR AND MONTH
2  ANNUAL INCOME          45000
3  ============================================================
4  CATEGORY        PERCENTAGE          ANNUAL    MONTH
5  ============================================================
6  HOUSING            0.3               13500     1125
7  FOOD               0.2                9000      750
8  TRANSPORTATION     0.1                4500      375
9  CLOTHING           0.1                4500      375
10 ENTERTAINMENT      0.3               13500     1125
11 ============================================================
12
```

Figure 2.25 When you change the numeric entry in cell C3 from 30000 to 45000, all the formulas that depend on this value are updated automatically. The annual and monthly budget amounts change as indicated.

sheet automatically recalculated is a major reason for using an electronic spreadsheet program.

Many people like to use worksheets as an experimental tool to help them study the impact of varying certain numerical values in the worksheet. For example, you could experiment with annual income to find out how much you would need to handle $900 per month in housing costs. Experiment by changing the annual income figure again. If the number you enter does not produce an even result when multiplied by the percentage, 1-2-3 will display as many decimal places as possible. Don't worry about this right now. You'll learn how to make the worksheet neater in the next chapter.

If you wish to save the new worksheet you have created in this section, follow the procedure for saving the worksheet described in the previous section. Press

```
/ F S
    |
    |──── Save
    └──── File
```

Line 2 of the control panel will display the prompt

```
Enter name of file to save: C:\123DATA\BUDGET.wk1
```

Since the worksheet was assigned a file name the last time you saved it, 1-2-3 inserts the current name of the file for you. If you wish to change that name, type in a new name; if you wish to accept the current name, press ⏎. It is important to note that if you save the current worksheet under the previous file name, the old worksheet will be lost. But if you save the current worksheet under a new file name, both the current worksheet and the previous worksheet will be available.

If you press ⏎ to accept the previous name, line 2 of the control panel will display the menu options

```
Cancel  Replace  Backup
```

Selecting Cancel will return you to READY mode without saving the file. Selecting Replace will save the current worksheet in the disk file BUDGET, replacing the previously saved worksheet. Selecting Backup will rename the file containing the previously saved worksheet to BUDGET.BAK and save the current worksheet in the file name BUDGET.WK1.

Since you will be using the original budget worksheet in the tutorial in Chapter 3, save this worksheet under a different file name (for example, BUDGETA). Type

    BUDGETA

As soon as you begin typing, the previous file name is removed, and the new file name inserted. Press ⏎, and this worksheet is saved under the file name BUDGETA.WK1.

> **Keystroke Summary: Edit cell contents**
>
> Locate: Cell pointer on cell to be modified
>
> Press: F2
>
> Edit: Change cell contents using the editing keys in Fig. 2.23
>
> Press: ⏎

Printing a Worksheet

In this section you'll print a copy of the worksheet shown in Fig. 2.25, using your printer. Before printing, you need to understand worksheet ranges.

Worksheet Ranges

Often, it is necessary to work with a portion of the worksheet at a time. A rectangular block of cells in a worksheet is called a **range**. For example, the middle of the table in Fig. 2.25 that includes rows 6 through 10 and columns A through F forms a range.

Earlier, you learned that cells are addressed by typing a column letter and row number such as B3. Ranges are addressed by typing the address of two cells on diagonally opposite corners of the range, separated by one or two periods. For example, the range referred to above is referenced as:

    A6.F10 or A10.F6 or F10.A6 or F6.A10

Generally, the first form, specifying the cell in upper left corner and the cell in lower right corner, is the most convenient to use. When typing a **range address**, use either one or two periods between the corner cell addresses, and do not leave any spaces. Either way, 1-2-3 displays range addresses with two periods between the corner cell addresses.

See whether you understand the idea of worksheet ranges by writing a range address that contains all the cells used in Fig. 2.25. One possible answer is A1.F11. A1 is the cell in the upper left corner, and F11 is the cell in the lower right corner of the desired range. Verify that the range addresses given below are correct.

Desired Range	Range Address
Column headings	A4.F4
Row headings	A6.A10
Cells containing formulas	E6.F10
Cells containing percentages	C6.C10
Cell C4	C4.C4

The concept of a range is extremely important. You will be required to enter a range address many times in future tutorials of this book.

Printing

Printing a worksheet is accomplished by using the 1-2-3 menu system. Press

```
/ P
 └── Print
```

to enter the menu system and select the Print option. Respond to the menu

```
Printer   File
```

by pressing P to choose the menu option of printing the worksheet on the Printer rather than on a disk File. You are now at the third level of menu options having to do with printing a worksheet (see line 2 of the control panel in Fig. 2.26). In Release 2.2 of 1-2-3 the worksheet is replaced by a table indicating the current print settings.

Press

```
R
 └── Range
```

to define the range of cells to be printed. Respond to the prompt on line 2 of the control panel,

```
Enter print range: A1
```

```
A1: 'BUDGET EXPENDITURE BY YEAR AND MONTH                                 MENU
Range Line  Page  Options  Clear  Align  Go  Quit
Specify a range to print
┌──────────────────────── Print Settings ─────────────────────────
│   Destination:   Printer
│
│   Range:
│
│   Header:
│   Footer:
│
│   Margins:
│     Left 4      Right 76    Top 2   Bottom 2
│
│   Borders:
│     Columns
│     Rows
│
│   Setup string:
│
│   Page length:   66
│
│   Output:        As-Displayed (Formatted)
```

Figure 2.26 After selecting the menu options to print a worksheet range on the printer, line 2 will display the print menu options and (in Release 2.2) the worksheet will be replaced by a table indicating the current print settings. First, choose option Range to specify the range address to be printed. Then choose option Go to commence printing. When finished, choose option Quit to return to READY mode.

by typing

> A1.F11

This range address specifies that all of the cells in the worksheet are to be printed. When you have correctly typed the range address, press

> ⏎

Rather than returning to READY mode, you will return to the third-level menu containing the printing options (Fig. 2.26). The print setting for Range will specify A1..F11.

Check your printer. It should be turned on and set to on-line mode. If you are using continuous-form paper, the perforation should be aligned appropriately. Once the printer is set correctly, press

> G
> └── Go

to commence printing the selected range of the worksheet. After the printing is completed, you will again return to the third level of menu options. Press

Q
   └── Quit

to return to READY mode.

    If you would like some additional practice, try following the procedure again, but define a different print range. For example, try the range A1.E11 and notice that the last column will be missing. Also, feel free to experiment with the Options menu choice to specify other print settings.

Keystroke Summary: Print a worksheet range

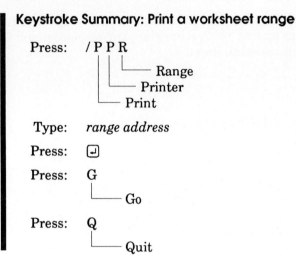

Press: / P P R
                    └── Range
               └── Printer
            └── Print

Type: *range address*

Press: ⏎

Press: G
            └── Go

Press: Q
            └── Quit

What Can Go Wrong?

1. You pressed G to begin printing, and the mode indicator says ERROR and the message "No print range specified" appears on line 25.

    Cause: A range address must be specified before attempting to print a worksheet.

    Solution: Press Esc to return to the third-level print menu. Press R and define a range address for printing followed by ⏎. Now press G.

2. You pressed G to begin printing, and after some delay the mode indicator says ERROR and the message "Printer error" appears on line 25.

    Cause: You may have forgotten to turn the printer on. The printer may be out of paper or in off-line mode. If you are using a T-switch, it may not be set to your computer.

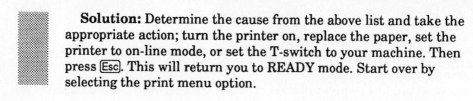

Solution: Determine the cause from the above list and take the appropriate action; turn the printer on, replace the paper, set the printer to on-line mode, or set the T-switch to your machine. Then press Esc. This will return you to READY mode. Start over by selecting the print menu option.

Exiting 1-2-3

This concludes the first tutorial. Be sure to save your current worksheet to disk whenever exiting 1-2-3; otherwise your worksheet will be lost.

To exit, use the menu system. Press

```
/ Q
  └─ Quit
```

Line 2 of the control panel will display the menu options

```
No  Yes
```

If you select Yes, you are confirming that you are ready to exit. The 1-2-3 program and your worksheet will be removed from memory. If you select No, you will not exit 1-2-3; instead, you'll return to your worksheet. This additional menu layer is designed to protect you from exiting 1-2-3 accidentally or before your worksheet has been saved. Press

```
Y
└─ Yes
```

to exit 1-2-3 and return to the operating system.

> **Keystroke Summary: Exit 1-2-3**
>
> Press:　/ Q Y
> 　　　　　　└─ Yes
> 　　　　└─ Quit

What Can Go Wrong?

1. After pressing / Q Y, you did not return to the operating system but returned to another 1-2-3 menu system called the access system.

Cause: You initially loaded 1-2-3 by using the command "lotus," which loaded 1-2-3 into memory through the access system.

Solution: Press E for menu option Exit followed by Y to confirm, Yes, that you wish to exit.

Summary

Function	Reference or Keystrokes	Page
Boot DOS	—	12
Cell entry, formula	Formula, ⏎	28
Cell entry, label	Label, ⏎	21
Cell entry, number	Number, ⏎	23
Cell pointer, move cursor	Fig. 2.4	18
Cell pointer, move direct	F5, cell address, ⏎	20
Edit cell contents	F2, Fig. 2.23	39
Exit 1-2-3	/ Q Y	46
File names	—	36
Label-prefix characters	Fig. 2.8	22
Load 1-2-3, floppy disk	—	14
Load 1-2-3, hard disk	—	15
Menu, access	/	31
Menu, back out	Esc	35
Menu, select method 1	→ or ←, ⏎	32
Menu, select method 2	First letter of menu option	34
Print a worksheet	/ P P R, range address, ⏎, G, Q	43
Range, definition	—	42
Save a worksheet	/ F S, file name, ⏎	36
Undo last operation	Alt *and* F4	27

Self-Test

1. How would you report today's date to DOS? _____ The current time? _____

2. The name of the 1-2-3 program is _____ .

3. The top three lines of the work screen are called the _____ .

4. The current worksheet cell is highlighted by the _____ .

5. The cell address of the upper left corner of the worksheet is _____ , and the cell address of the third row and fifth column is _____ .

6. The initial worksheet screen displays _____ rows and _____ columns.

7. Indicate the key (or keys) that move the cell pointer:

   a. one position to the right _____

   b. 20 rows down _____

   c. one screen to the right _____

   d. immediately to the upper left corner _____

8. A worksheet cell may contain a _____ , a _____ , or a _____ .

9. Labels are preceded by a _____ to indicate how the label is to be positioned in the cell.

10. When entering a number or a formula into a worksheet cell, the mode indicator will be set to _____ .

11. The following label entry will fill a cell with minus signs: _____ .

12. The following formula entry will add the values in cells A1 and A2: _____ .

13. The following formula entry will average the values in cells A1 and A2: _____ .

14. Press _____ to bring up the 1-2-3 menu system.

15. Press _____ to select the File option from the main menu.

16. Press _____ to save a worksheet in the file named SALES.

17. Press _____ to edit the contents of the highlighted cell.

18. In EDIT mode the _____ key moves the edit cursor to the end of the line.

19. In general, the _____ key is used to return to a previous state without taking any action, and the _____ key is used to complete an action.

20. Indicate a range address for each block of cells:

    a. Rows 2–5 and columns 1–3 _____

    b. 5 rows and 5 columns in the upper left corner _____

21. Press _____ to define the range A1.B5 for printing.

22. Press _____ to print the defined range.

23. Press _____ to exit 1-2-3.

Exercises

1. Print two worksheets that you created by following the tutorial in this chapter, and submit them to your instructor. One worksheet should be based on an annual income figure of 30000, and the other should be based on 45000.

2. Use 1-2-3 to create a worksheet representing a college student budget. Use a format similar to the one following. Treat the annual expenditure, annual tuition, annual housing, and annual book figures as numbers. The annual entertainment is a formula that computes the amount left over after expenses in the other categories. Use a formula for all the monthly expenditures. Save and print the completed worksheet.

```
COLLEGE BUDGET
ANNUAL EXPENDITURE      9600
===================================
CATEGORY           ANNUAL   MONTH
===================================
TUITION              4800     400
HOUSING              3000     250
BOOKS                 600      50
ENTERTAIN            1200     100
===================================
```

3. Use 1-2-3 to create a worksheet to compute a batting average and slugging average as illustrated below. The number of each type of hit and outs are entered as numbers. A formula is used to total the number of at bats. The batting average is computed by using a formula dividing the total number of hits by the total number of times at bat. The slugging average counts a home run as 4 hits, a triple as 3 hits, a double as 2 hits, and a single as 1 hit in computing the batting average. You might wish to enhance this worksheet to include walks, different types of outs, and other batting occurrences. Save and print the completed worksheet.

```
BATTING AVERAGE COMPUTATION
============================
RESULT             TIMES
============================
SINGLE               12
DOUBLE                4
TRIPLE                2
HOME RUN              2
============================
OUT                  41
============================
TOTAL AT BATS        61
============================
BATTING AVERAGE    0.327868
SLUGGING AVERAGE   0.557377
```

3

Modifying a Worksheet

This chapter introduces the 1-2-3 features and commands that allow you to:

- retrieve a worksheet

- delete rows and/or columns from a worksheet

- insert additional rows and/or columns in a worksheet

- adjust column widths

- adjust the label-prefix character in a worksheet range

- fix the number of decimal places

- include % and $ symbols with numeric values

- erase portions or all of a worksheet

Overview

In Chapter 2 you learned to modify a worksheet by editing the contents of individual cells. If you have many changes to make, this can be a very tedious process. In this chapter you will learn some powerful methods for modifying many cells of a worksheet at the same time.

```
             A            B            C          D           E
1  BUDGET EXPENDITURE BY YEAR AND MONTH
2  ANNUAL INCOME        $30,000
3  ===================================================================
4  CATEGORY       PERCENTAGE     ANNUAL    QUARTERLY    MONTHLY
5  ===================================================================
6  HOUSING             30%      $9,000     $2,250        $750
7  FOOD                20%      $6,000     $1,500        $500
8  TRANSPORTATION      10%      $3,000       $750        $250
9  OTHER               40%     $12,000     $3,000      $1,000
10 ===================================================================
11
12
```

Figure 3.1 This is the finished worksheet that you will be creating in the tutorial presented in this chapter.

Specifically, in this tutorial you'll retrieve the example worksheet you saved in Chapter 2 and modify it. After you have completed the tutorial in this chapter, the worksheet will appear as in Fig. 3.1. Notice the modifications that will have taken place:

1. Previously blank columns are deleted.

2. The budget categories CLOTHING and ENTERTAINMENT are consolidated into a single category OTHER.

3. Column spacing is achieved by adjusting column widths.

4. An additional column QUARTERLY is added to the worksheet.

5. The column headings ANNUAL, QUARTERLY, and MONTHLY are aligned with the right edge of the cells.

6. The dollar figures for annual income and budget amounts in each category are formatted with dollar signs and commas.

7. The percentages are formatted with % signs.

When you are ready to begin the tutorial, follow the procedures outlined in Chapter 2 to boot the operating system and load 1-2-3.

Retrieving a Worksheet

If you have properly loaded 1-2-3, you'll see an empty worksheet on the screen. Begin this tutorial by reading into memory the personal budget worksheet you saved in Chapter 2. This will allow you to make modifications to the worksheet. Recall that this worksheet is stored in a disk file named BUDGET.

Name of file to retrieve: C:\123DATA*.wk?
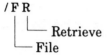   BUDGETA.WK1

Figure 3.2 After choosing the menu options / F R, you are prompted to select the name of the file to retrieve. Use ⊡ or ⊡ to highlight the file name BUDGET, and press ⏎.

To ask 1-2-3 to read the worksheet from a disk file, use the menu system. Press

/ F R
└── Retrieve
└─ File

to select primary menu option File and secondary menu option Retrieve. (Recall that you are encouraged to select menu options by highlighting the desired option and pressing ⏎, even though the tutorial instructs you to press the first letter of the desired options.) The control panel is shown in Fig. 3.2. Line 2 indicates that the file will be retrieved from the hard disk (drive C) and the directory named 123DATA. If you are retrieving the file from a floppy disk in drive B, line 2 reads,

Name of file to retrieve: B:*.wk?

Line 3 of the control panel contains a list of all of the worksheet files (those with an extension beginning with the letters wk) in the given directory.

At this point, 1-2-3 is in FILES mode and is waiting for you to select the name of the disk file to be retrieved. The first file name on line 3 is highlighted. To select a file name, use ⊡ or ⊡ to mark the file name desired and then press ⏎. In your case the desired file name is BUDGET. Highlight this file and press ⏎. After a brief delay, the worksheet stored in the disk file BUDGET is copied into memory and displayed on the screen for you to modify (Fig. 3.3).

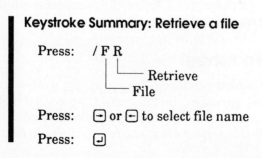

Keystroke Summary: Retrieve a file

Press: / F R
└── Retrieve
└─ File

Press: ⊡ or ⊡ to select file name

Press: ⏎

```
       A        B         C        D       E        F       G        H
1  BUDGET EXPENDITURE BY YEAR AND MONTH
2  ANNUAL INCOME        30000
3  =================================================================
4  CATEGORY             PERCENTAGE        ANNUAL   MONTHLY
5  =================================================================
6  HOUSING              0.3               9000     750
7  FOOD                 0.2               6000     500
8  TRANSPORTATION       0.1               3000     250
9  CLOTHING             0.1               3000     250
10 ENTERTAINMENT        0.3               9000     750
11 =================================================================
12
```

Figure 3.3 After retrieval of the worksheet stored in the disk file BUDGET, your 1-2-3 screen will look like this.

What Can Go Wrong?

1. You are using a floppy disk system. After choosing the menu option to retrieve a file, a brief delay occurs, and you receive the error message "Disk drive not ready" at the bottom of the screen.

Cause: 1-2-3 is trying to read the names of the worksheet files stored on the floppy disk in drive B, but no disk is there.

Solution: Place the data disk you used to store the BUDGET worksheet in drive B. Press (Esc) to return to READY mode and start over.

2. The worksheet file BUDGET does not appear on line 3 of the control panel.

Cause: When 1-2-3 was initially set up on your hard disk system, a certain directory (the default directory) was established as the place where worksheet files are to be stored. These settings are indicated on line 2 of the control panel. Your BUDGET file is stored in a different directory. Or, on a floppy disk system, you have the wrong data disk in drive B.

Solution: In the first case, change the default directory as described in the section entitled SAVING THE WORKSHEET. Or if the directory name you wish is displayed on line 3 (directory names are followed by the \ character), use ⊡ or ⊡ to highlight that name and press ⏎. This will display the worksheet files in that directory on line 3. In the second case, place the correct data disk in drive B, press (Esc) until you return to READY mode, and start over.

Deleting Rows and/or Columns

Now that you have retrieved the worksheet, look at it carefully. Notice that the cells in columns B and D contain no labels, values, or formulas other than the equals signs used to define worksheet boundaries in rows 3, 5, and 11. These columns were left blank intentionally to provide spacing in the table. Later in this chapter you will learn to adjust the width of individual columns so you'll no longer need these extra columns for spacing. Delete them.

To delete column B, position the cell pointer in any row of column B and choose the Worksheet menu option by pressing

/ W
└─ Worksheet

Line 2 of the control panel (Fig. 3.4) lists the Worksheet menu options that provide choices for modifying the worksheet. You'll be using the first five options in this chapter (Fig. 3.5). Use ⊟ and ⊟ to highlight each of these options and compare the descriptions on line 3 of the control panel with the descriptions in Fig. 3.5.

To continue with the example, press

D
└─ Delete

The menu options will appear on line 2 of the control panel:

        Column   Row

One deletes columns; the other deletes rows. Press C. The prompt

        Enter range of columns to delete: B1..B1

appears. At this point you are to define a range address that includes the columns to be deleted. Since you initially positioned the cell pointer in column B, 1-2-3 suggests a range address that includes the single column B (B1..B1). If you wanted to delete columns B through F, you would type a range address that included these columns, for example, B1.F1 or B2.F5. In your case you

---

B1:   MENU
Global Insert Delete Column Erase Titles Window Status Page Learn
Format Label-Prefix Column-Width Recalculation Protection Default Zero

Figure 3.4 The Worksheet menu options are listed on line 2 of the control panel. All these options involve modifications to the worksheet. Use ⊟ or ⊟ to highlight each option, and read the description on line 3.

Menu Choice	Provides Options for
Global	setting default format, label-prefix, column width, and other worksheet characteristics
Insert	inserting additional rows or columns
Delete	deleting rows or columns
Column	setting the width and other characteristics of a column
Erase	erasing the worksheet

Figure 3.5 The Worksheet option in 1-2-3 provides options for modifying the worksheet. This chapter involves options in the first five groups.

wish to delete only column B, so the suggested range address is fine. Do not type anything.

Press ⏎. The contents of all cells in column B are deleted, and the rest of the worksheet moves over to fill in the free space (Fig. 3.6). The contents of the cells in column C have moved to B, the contents of the cells in column D have moved to C, and so on.

Note that some of the labels in column A have been truncated; for example, see ANNUAL IN in cell A2. That's because column B no longer contains empty cells. The entire label, ANNUAL INCOME, is still stored in cell A2, but the column to the right is not empty. Therefore the label is truncated to fit into the nine spaces available to display the contents of cells in column A. You will learn to adjust the column width later in this chapter.

```
 B1:                                                                  READY

         A          B          C          D          E       F       G          H
1   BUDGET EXPENDITURE BY YEAR AND MONTH
2   ANNUAL IN     30000
3   ============================================
4   CATEGORY PERCENTAGE            ANNUAL    MONTHLY
5   ============================================
6   HOUSING       0.3              9000      750
7   FOOD          0.2              6000      500
8   TRANSPORT     0.1              3000      250
9   CLOTHING      0.1              3000      250
10  ENTERTAIN     0.3              9000      750
11  ============================================
12
```

Figure 3.6 After deletion of column B, the contents of columns C, D, E, and F move one column to the left.

Modifying a Worksheet
Deleting Rows and/or Columns

```
       A         B        C        D        E      F      G      H
1  BUDGET EXPENDITURE BY YEAR AND MONTH
2  ANNUAL IN    30000
3  ========================================================
4  CATEGORY  PERCENTAGE           ANNUAL   MONTHLY
5  ========================================================
6  HOUSING       0.3              9000     750
7  FOOD          0.2              6000     500
8  TRANSPORT     0.1              3000     250
9  CLOTHING      0.1              3000     250
10 ENTERTAIN     0.3              9000     750
11 ========================================================
12
```

Figure 3.7 When columns are deleted and the following columns are moved over, cells containing formulas are automatically adjusted. The formula in cell D6 was originally in cell E6, and the original formula was +C2*C6. Since the contents of column C moved to column B, the formula was automatically changed to +B2*B6.

Note also the formulas. Position the cell pointer over cell D6 (Fig. 3.7). Notice that the formula for the annual housing budget is appropriately adjusted to +B2*B6. You originally entered the formula as +C2*C6 in Chapter 2, but since column B was deleted and column C moved over, the formula has been adjusted automatically by 1-2-3.

Follow the same procedure to delete column C. Position the cell pointer to any row in column C. Sequentially, press / W D C to choose the menu option to delete a column. You'll be prompted to enter a range address that includes the columns you wish to delete. The suggested range address will contain the single column, C. Press ⏎ to accept the suggested address. As before, the contents of the cells in columns D and E move one column to the left, and the formulas are adjusted automatically. Your worksheet now looks like Fig. 3.8.

Review Fig. 3.1 again. Note that the last two budget categories, CLOTH-ING and ENTERTAINMENT, are consolidated into a single category called OTHER. This is accomplished by deleting the CLOTHING row from the worksheet and then editing the category label and percentage number of the ENTERTAINMENT row.

First, delete row 9. The process is almost identical to deleting a column. Position the cell pointer to any column in row 9. Press

```
       A         B         C         D     E      F      G      H
1  BUDGET EXPENDITURE BY YEAR AND MONTH
2  ANNUAL IN     30000
3  ===================================
4  CATEGORY PERCENTAGANNUAL    MONTHLY
5  ===================================
6  HOUSING        0.3      9000      750
7  FOOD           0.2      6000      500
8  TRANSPORT      0.1      3000      250
9  CLOTHING       0.1      3000      250
10 ENTERTAIN      0.3      9000      750
11 ===================================
12
```

Figure 3.8 After deleting column C from the worksheet in Fig. 3.7, you obtain this worksheet.

to choose the menu option to delete a row. You will be prompted as follows:

```
    Enter range of rows to delete: A9..A9
```

Since you initially highlighted a cell in row 9, the suggested range address includes that single row. As with columns, you may type in a different range address that includes all the rows you wish to delete. In your case you wish to delete only row 9, so press ⏎ to accept the suggested range address.

The worksheet now appears as in Fig. 3.9. The contents of the cells in rows below row 9 have moved up one row. As before, formulas are automatically adjusted as necessary.

```
       A         B         C         D     E      F      G      H
1  BUDGET EXPENDITURE BY YEAR AND MONTH
2  ANNUAL IN     30000
3  ===================================
4  CATEGORY PERCENTAGANNUAL    MONTHLY
5  ===================================
6  HOUSING        0.3      9000      750
7  FOOD           0.2      6000      500
8  TRANSPORT      0.1      3000      250
9  ENTERTAIN      0.3      9000      750
10 ===================================
11
12
```

Figure 3.9 After deletion of row 9, the contents of row 10 are moved up to fill in row 9.

Modifying a Worksheet   **57**
Deleting Rows and/or Columns

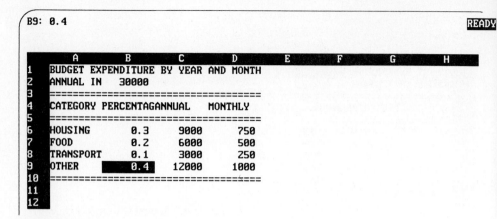

	A	B	C	D	E	F	G	H
1	BUDGET EXPENDITURE BY YEAR AND MONTH							
2	ANNUAL IN	30000						
3	==================================							
4	CATEGORY	PERCENTAG	ANNUAL	MONTHLY				
5	==================================							
6	HOUSING	0.3	9000	750				
7	FOOD	0.2	6000	500				
8	TRANSPORT	0.1	3000	250				
9	OTHER	0.4	12000	1000				
10	==================================							
11								
12								

Figure 3.10 After editing the label in cell A9 and the number in cell B9, you obtain this worksheet.

To complete the consolidation of the last two budget categories in your worksheet, edit the category in cell A9 to contain the label, OTHER, and change the percentage in cell B9 to 0.4 (Fig. 3.10). Do this by positioning the cell pointer on the respective cells and either reentering the cell contents or pressing F2 and modifying the existing cell contents. If you've forgotten how to do this, review the section on modifying a worksheet cell in Chapter 2.

Keystroke Summary: Delete rows or columns

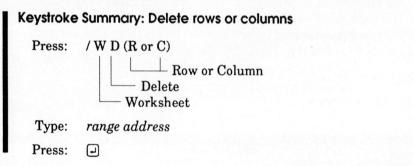

Press: / W D (R or C)
                            Row or Column
                        Delete
                    Worksheet

Type: *range address*

Press: ⏎

What Can Go Wrong?

1. You accidentally deleted the wrong columns or rows from your worksheet.

Cause: The range address that you specified contained the wrong columns or rows. Remember that when you are deleting columns (or rows), all columns (rows) in the specified range will be deleted.

Solution: If you are using Release 2.2 and have performed no other operations since your mistake, the simplest procedure is to press the UNDO key ([Alt] *and* [F4]). Otherwise, you'll need to start over by retrieving the BUDGET file again. The original worksheet from disk will replace the modified worksheet, and you can retrace your steps. See the previous section to retrieve a worksheet. Incidentally, it is good practice to save your worksheet to disk periodically so that if something goes wrong, you can retrieve it.

Inserting Rows and/or Columns

In the last section you learned how to delete rows or columns from a worksheet. Similarly, 1-2-3 commands allow you to move in the opposite direction; that is, you can create additional space in a worksheet by inserting blank rows or columns. In the modified worksheet, illustrated in Fig. 3.1, an additional column containing the QUARTERLY budget amounts is inserted between the ANNUAL and MONTHLY columns. This is accomplished by inserting a blank column between the ANNUAL and MONTHLY columns and then entering labels, numbers, and formulas into the new column as appropriate.

To insert a blank column to the left of column D, position the cell pointer to any cell in column D. Choose the menu option,

```
/ W I
    └── Insert
    └── Worksheet
```

You'll then be given the menu options

```
Column Row
```

Press C to indicate that you wish to insert blank columns. You will be prompted as follows:

```
Enter column insert range: D1..D1
```

Enter a range address that contains the columns you wish to insert; any information that is already in these columns will be moved over as appropriate. The suggested address contains the single column D, since you positioned the cell pointer in this column when you chose this menu option. Press ⏎ to accept this range address and to insert a single blank column (Fig. 3.11). Note that the contents of cells previously in column D are moved to column E, and a blank column is inserted. Any formulas affected by the change are automatically adjusted.

Now enter the appropriate labels and formulas into the cells of column D. This column contains quarterly budget expenditures and uses labels and

```
        A          B          C          D        E        F        G        H
1   BUDGET EXPENDITURE BY YEAR AND MONTH
2   ANNUAL IN     30000
3   =================================        =========
4   CATEGORY PERCENTAGANNUAL                 MONTHLY
5   =================================        =========
6   HOUSING        0.3       9000                 750
7   FOOD           0.2       6000                 500
8   TRANSPORT      0.1       3000                 250
9   OTHER          0.4      12000                1000
10  =================================        =========
11
12
```

Figure 3.11 After a blank column is inserted in column D, the previous contents of column D are shifted to column E.

formulas that are analogous to those you entered for the MONTHLY column in Chapter 2. Cells D3, D5, and D10 contain the label \= (recall that \ is a label-prefix character indicating that the following character, =, is to be repeated across the entire cell width) to provide a worksheet boundary. Cell D4 contains the column heading QUARTERLY. Cells D6 through D9 contain formulas to compute the quarterly budget available in each category. This is computed by taking the annual budget amount and dividing by 4. For example, the formula in cell D6 is +C6/4. Enter similar formulas in cells D7 through D9. After you have entered all the information in the new column, the worksheet will appear as in Fig. 3.12.

```
        A          B          C          D        E        F        G        H
1   BUDGET EXPENDITURE BY YEAR AND MONTH
2   ANNUAL IN     30000
3   =================================================
4   CATEGORY PERCENTAGANNUAL      QUARTERLYMONTHLY
5   =================================================
6   HOUSING        0.3       9000      2250       750
7   FOOD           0.2       6000      1500       500
8   TRANSPORT      0.1       3000       750       250
9   OTHER          0.4      12000      3000      1000
10  =================================================
11
12
```

Figure 3.12 Labels and formulas are entered in the cells of the newly created column D to obtain this worksheet.

Inserting additional blank rows in the worksheet is almost identical to inserting columns. The tutorial example does not require any additional rows; but for practice, insert 3 additional rows between the budget categories FOOD and TRANSPORTATION and then delete them.

Position the cell pointer in cell A8 and choose the menu option,

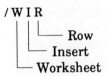

to insert additional blank rows above row 8. The prompt on line 2 reads:

```
Enter row insert range: A8..A8
```

Type

A8.A10

to insert 3 blank rows (rows 8, 9, and 10). Press ⏎. Three blank rows are inserted, and the last three rows of the worksheet are moved down.

Since this was just for practice, delete these three rows to return to the worksheet in Fig. 3.12. Position the cell pointer to cell A8. Press / W D R to choose the menu option to delete worksheet rows. Type the range address A8.A10 to specify that rows 8 to 10 are to be deleted, and press ⏎.

Keystroke Summary: Insert rows or columns

Press: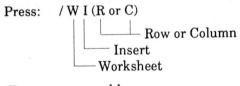

Type: *range address*

Press: ⏎

What Can Go Wrong?

1. You accidentally inserted columns or rows in the wrong position of your worksheet.

Cause: The range address that you specified contained the wrong columns or rows. Remember that when you are inserting columns (or rows), blank columns (rows) will be inserted in each column (row) of the specified range.

Solution: Either use the UNDO key (Alt *and* F4) or delete the newly inserted columns (rows) and start the procedure over. See the previous section to delete columns (rows) from a worksheet.

2. After you have entered a range address, the mode indicator flashes ERROR, and line 25 contains the message "Invalid cell or range address."

Cause: The range address you typed contains an erroneous character.

Solution: Press [Esc] to return to READY mode. Start the procedure over. Remember that a proper range address is composed of a cell address, one or two periods, and another cell address. Leave no blanks. This type of error can occur in any procedure requiring a range address.

Adjusting Column Widths

Initially, the width of each column of a worksheet is set to nine spaces, but you can adjust the column width to allow appropriate spacing between columns of the worksheet. In your example worksheet (Fig. 3.12) the columns need to be widened to allow additional space for certain labels (for example, ANNUAL IN, PERCENTAG, and TRANSPORT). In this section you will learn to adjust the width of all columns or a single column.

Adjusting the Width of All Columns

When a worksheet is initially created, certain global worksheet characteristics are established, such as the default label-prefix character, the default number format (to be discussed later in this chapter), and the default column width. To change the global settings, press

```
/ W G
    |  └─ Global
    └─ Worksheet
```

A new menu will appear, and if you are using Release 2.2, the worksheet will be replaced by a table containing the current global settings (Fig. 3.13); each option on this menu allows you to change one of the default settings of the worksheet. Use ⊟ to highlight each option on the menu, and read the description on line 3 to get a feel for the choices provided.

To change the global column width, press

```
C
 └─ Column-Width
```

The worksheet will reappear, and you will be prompted (Fig. 3.14) as follows:

```
Enter global column width (1..240): 9
```

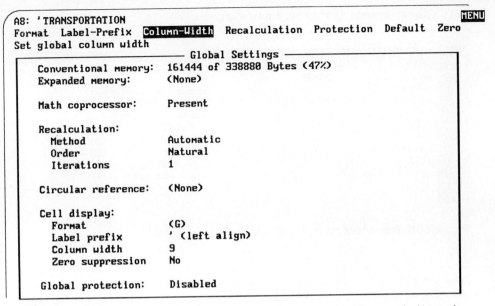

```
A8: 'TRANSPORTATION                                          MENU
Format  Label-Prefix  Column-Width  Recalculation  Protection  Default  Zero
Set global column width
┌───────────────────── Global Settings ─────────────────────┐
│  Conventional memory:   161444 of 338880 Bytes (47%)       │
│  Expanded memory:       (None)                             │
│                                                            │
│  Math coprocessor:      Present                            │
│                                                            │
│  Recalculation:                                            │
│    Method               Automatic                          │
│    Order                Natural                            │
│    Iterations           1                                  │
│                                                            │
│  Circular reference:    (None)                             │
│                                                            │
│  Cell display:                                             │
│    Format               (G)                                │
│    Label prefix         ' (left align)                     │
│    Column width         9                                  │
│    Zero suppression     No                                 │
│                                                            │
│  Global protection:     Disabled                           │
└────────────────────────────────────────────────────────────┘
```

Figure 3.13 After the menu options / W G are chosen, line 2 of the control panel provides menu options for setting default values for the worksheet, and the worksheet is replaced by a table of global settings. The option Column-Width is highlighted. Choose this option to specify the number of spaces allocated to each column in the worksheet.

The default column width 9 is provided. At this point you could type the desired column width and press ⏎. However, don't. This is a good place to introduce POINT mode.

Note that the mode indicator says POINT. This is an indication that the desired input may be obtained by pointing with the cursor keys rather than typing the desired value. Press ⊡ once and the column width increases to 10; the change is reflected on the screen. Press ⊡ again and the column width increases another unit. Each time ⊡ is pressed, the column width increases by one unit, and the change is displayed on the screen. Pressing ⊟ decreases the column width by one unit. Press ⊡ and ⊟ several times so that you see

```
A1: 'BUDGET EXPENDITURE BY YEAR AND MONTH                    POINT
Enter global column width (1..240): 9
```

Figure 3.14 Use ⊡ to increase the column width and ⊟ to decrease it. Press ⏎ when you are satisfied with the setting.

```
           A            B            C            D            E            F
 1  BUDGET EXPENDITURE BY YEAR AND MONTH
 2  ANNUAL INCOM      30000
 3  =================================================================
 4  CATEGORY     PERCENTAGE  ANNUAL      QUARTERLY    MONTHLY
 5  =================================================================
 6  HOUSING            0.3        9000         2250          750
 7  FOOD               0.2        6000         1500          500
 8  TRANSPORTATI       0.1        3000          750          250
 9  OTHER              0.4       12000         3000         1000
10  =================================================================
11
12
```

Figure 3.15 The global column width is set to 12 spaces.

how pointing works. Notice that as the column width decreases, more columns appear on the screen; as the column width increases, fewer columns appear on the screen.

Use ⊡ or ⊟ to select a column width of 12. Press ⏎ to confirm your choice. Each column on your worksheet is now 12 spaces wide (Fig. 3.15). Notice that the labels ANNUAL INCOME and TRANSPORTATION are still truncated; clearly, 12 spaces is not enough for column A. You'll correct this in the next section.

Keystroke Summary: Adjust the width of all columns

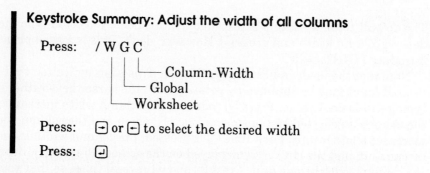

Press: / W G C
                    └── Column-Width
                  └── Global
                └── Worksheet

Press: ⊡ or ⊟ to select the desired width

Press: ⏎

Adjusting the Width of a Single Column

The procedure described above is useful to change the default column width setting for all columns in the worksheet. However, it is frequently desirable to set each column individually to allow for variable-width columns.

To illustrate, set the width of column A to 16 spaces. Position the cell pointer in column A and press

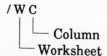

/ W C
        └── Column
      └── Worksheet

to access a menu of choices for setting parameters of the column containing
the cell pointer:

```
Set-Width   Reset-Width   Hide   Display   Column-Range
```

Press S to set the column width. You will then be prompted as follows:

```
Enter column width (1..240): 12
```

This time the column width you choose applies only to this single column.

Press ⊟ four times until the column width equals 16, and then press ⏎
(Fig. 3.16). Notice line 1 of the control panel. In addition to the usual display
of cell contents, line 1 contains the symbol [W16]. This indicates that the
width of this column is set to 16 spaces.

Next, set the width of column B to ten spaces. Position the cell pointer on
column B. Sequentially, press / W C S. Press ⊟ twice to set the column width
to ten, press ⏎, and note the changes in the worksheet (Fig. 3.17).

In summary, the menu option / W G C sets the column width of all columns in the worksheet, and the menu option / W C S *overrides* this setting
for an individual column. Release 2.2 of 1-2-3 also provides a feature for
overriding the column width setting for a group of columns (/ W C C).

> ### Keystroke Summary: Adjust the width of a single column
>
> Press: / W C S
>   │ │ └─── Set-Width
>   │ └──── Column
>   └───── Worksheet
>
> Press: ⊟ or ⊟ to select the desired width
>
> Press: ⏎

```
A1: [W16] 'BUDGET EXPENDITURE BY YEAR AND MONTH                        READY

            A          B          C          D          E
1  BUDGET EXPENDITURE BY YEAR AND MONTH
2  ANNUAL INCOME        30000
3  ==================================================================
4  CATEGORY        PERCENTAGE  ANNUAL      QUARTERLY   MONTHLY
5  ==================================================================
6  HOUSING              0.3       9000        2250         750
7  FOOD                 0.2       6000        1500         500
8  TRANSPORTATION       0.1       3000         750         250
9  OTHER                0.4      12000        3000        1000
10 ==================================================================
11
12
```

Figure 3.16 The width of column A is set to 16 spaces.

```
                A             B          C           D          E
1   BUDGET EXPENDITURE BY YEAR AND MONTH
2   ANNUAL INCOME        30000
3   ================================================================
4   CATEGORY        PERCENTAGEANNUAL     QUARTERLY   MONTHLY
5   ================================================================
6   HOUSING              0.3       9000        2250        750
7   FOOD                 0.2       6000        1500        500
8   TRANSPORTATION       0.1       3000         750        250
9   OTHER                0.4      12000        3000       1000
10  ================================================================
11
12
```

Figure 3.17 The width of column B is set to 10 spaces.

What Can Go Wrong?

1. You set the width of the wrong column to 10 or 16.

Cause: The cell pointer was positioned in the wrong column when you followed the procedure to set the column width.

Solution: UNDO the last operation using Alt *and* F4 or reset the column width of the incorrect column to the default value. Position the cell pointer on this column and choose the following menu options:

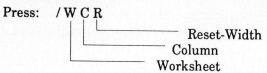

Adjusting Label-Prefix Characters

Review the current version of your worksheet (Fig. 3.17). Notice that all the column heading labels are aligned with the left edge of their cells. Recall from Chapter 2 that when you entered these labels, they were automatically preceded by the default label-prefix character, ', which specifies this alignment. In most cases, left alignment is fine, but your worksheet would look better if the column headings ANNUAL, QUARTERLY, and MONTHLY were aligned with the right edge of the cell. This can be accomplished by editing each of these cells individually to replace the label-prefix character ' with " or by changing the label-prefix characters of an entire range of cells at once.

```
C4: 'ANNUAL                                                            MENU
Format  Label  Erase  Name  Justify  Prot  Unprot  Input  Value  Trans  Search
Fixed  Sci  Currency  ,  General  +/-  Percent  Date  Text  Hidden  Reset
```

Figure 3.18 After choosing the menu option / R, you obtain the menu options listed on line 2 of the control panel. All of these options involve modifications to a part (or range) of the worksheet. Use ⊟ or ⊟ to highlight each option and read the description on line 3.

Position the cell pointer on cell C4 and choose the Range menu option:

/ R
└─ Range

The Range option provides a number of menu choices for modifying portions or ranges of the worksheet (Fig. 3.18). In this chapter you will be using the first three options (Fig. 3.19). Use ⊟ and ⊟ to highlight each of these options, and compare the descriptions on line 3 of the control panel with the descriptions in Fig. 3.19.

To continue with the example, press

L
└─ Label

to select the option for modifying the label-prefix characters. Line 2 of the control panel will display the following menu choices:

```
Left   Right   Center
```

Press R to select alignment with the right edge of the cell.

You will then be prompted to enter the range address of the labels to modify:

```
Enter range of labels: C4..C4
```

Menu Choice	Provides Options for
Format	determining the appearance or format of numbers in the worksheet
Label	modifying the label-prefix character of a range of worksheet cells
Erase	erasing the contents of a range of worksheet cells

Figure 3.19 The Range option in 1-2-3 provides options for modifying a specified range of the worksheet. This chapter involves options in the first three groups.

Modifying a Worksheet   **67**
Adjusting Label-Prefix Characters

Type a range address that contains all the labels you wish to align with the right edge of the cell. If the range address includes cells with numbers or formulas, they will not be affected because the label-prefix character does not apply to worksheet values; it applies only to labels. In your example, type

C4.E4

to modify the alignment of the last three column labels. Press ⏎, and watch the worksheet change (Fig. 3.20). Position the cell pointer over each of these column labels and notice that the prefix character displayed on line 1 of the control panel is " to indicate the right edge alignment of the label in that cell.

Keystroke Summary: Adjust the label-prefix character in a range

Press: / R L (L or R or C)
├── Left, Right, or Center
├── Label
└── Range

Type: *range address*

Press: ⏎

What Can Go Wrong?

1. You aligned labels other than the three column headings desired with the right edge of the cell.

Cause: You entered the wrong range address.

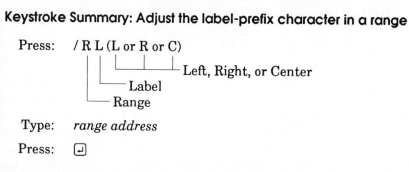

```
C4: "ANNUAL                                                              READY

          A              B              C         D            E
1  BUDGET EXPENDITURE BY YEAR AND MONTH
2  ANNUAL INCOME          30000
3  ============================================================
4  CATEGORY          PERCENTAGE       ANNUAL   QUARTERLY    MONTHLY
5  ============================================================
6  HOUSING               0.3           9000      2250        750
7  FOOD                  0.2           6000      1500        500
8  TRANSPORTATION        0.1           3000       750        250
9  OTHER                 0.4          12000      3000       1000
10 ============================================================
11
12
```

Figure 3.20 The column labels ANNUAL, QUARTERLY, and MONTHLY are aligned with the right edge of the cell.

Solution: Use the procedures in this section to adjust the label-prefix character of the incorrect labels. After pressing / R L, choose option L to align the labels with the left edge of the cell. Carefully enter the desired range address. If you modified the label-prefix character of any cells containing repeating equal signs, you'll need to edit each of these cells individually.

2. The three column headings are still aligned with the left edge of the cell, or they are centered in the cell.

Cause: You chose the wrong alignment option.

Solution: Start over again. After pressing / R L, choose option R to align the labels with the right edge of the cell. L aligns labels with the left edge and C aligns labels in the center.

Note: The UNDO key combination ([Alt] *and* [F4]) may often be used to solve a problem identified in the "What Can Go Wrong?" feature *if* the problem occurs as a result of the last operation. For the remaining 1-2-3 tutorials this option will not be suggested as a possible solution. Instead, the "What Can Go Wrong?" features will assume that you have tried UNDO and are looking for a different solution.

Formatting Worksheet Values

1-2-3 provides several options for specifying how numeric values, including numbers and formulas, appear on the worksheet. Though 1-2-3 stores values with a precision of 15 decimal places, you may control the number of decimal places displayed and the formatting of these numeric values. In this section of the tutorial, you will learn some of these **format** options and will modify the numeric values in the worksheet to display zero decimal places and to include dollar signs and percent signs where appropriate.

Format Options

1-2-3 provides many format options. The most common are Fixed, Currency, Comma, General, and Percent. All but the General option allow you to specify the number of decimal places displayed.

Numeric values are always aligned with the right edge of the worksheet cell. If the column width is not sufficient to display the numeric value (including an extra space for the % sign) in the specified format, asterisks appear across the width of the cell. Some examples are provided in Fig. 3.21 to illustrate the various formatting options. In each case it is assumed that the column width is set to ten spaces. The Fixed format sets the number of decimal places, the Currency format adds dollar signs and commas, the

Internal Value	Format Option	Displayed Value
1234	Fixed, 2 decimal places	1234.00
1234.567	Currency, 0 decimal places	$1,235
1234.567	General	1234.567
1234567	Comma, 0 decimal places	1,234,567
123456789	Comma, 0 decimal places	**********
.1234	Percent, 1 decimal place	12.3%

Figure 3.21 Examples are provided to illustrate how the format options Fixed, Currency, Comma, Percent, and General display various numeric values in a column width of ten spaces.

Comma format just adds commas, and the Percent format multiplies the internal value by 100 and adds a percent sign. Normally, numeric values are displayed using the General format. This displays the value to as many decimal places as possible.

Formatting for numeric values may be specified for the entire worksheet by adjusting the default format setting, or it may be specified for a particular range of the worksheet. Each of these approaches is illustrated.

Formatting Values Throughout the Entire Worksheet

Consider the numeric values in the example worksheet (Fig. 3.20). Most of these numbers represent dollar figures, and nearest dollar accuracy is sufficient for budgeting purposes. Therefore it is reasonable to change these numbers to the Currency format and to display zero decimal places.

Choose the menu option that allows you to change the global format setting:

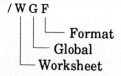

The worksheet is replaced with the global settings table, and line 2 of the control panel lists the available format choices:

```
Fixed  Sci  Currency  ,  General  +/-  Percent  Date  Text  Hidden
```

Press C to select Currency. The prompt

```
        Enter number of decimal places (0..15): 2
```

appears on line 2. Type

```
   0
```

```
            A          B          C          D          E
1  BUDGET EXPENDITURE BY YEAR AND MONTH
2  ANNUAL INCOME      $30,000
3  =============================================================
4  CATEGORY        PERCENTAGE     ANNUAL    QUARTERLY     MONTHLY
5  =============================================================
6  HOUSING             $0        $9,000      $2,250        $750
7  FOOD                $0        $6,000      $1,500        $500
8  TRANSPORTATION      $0        $3,000        $750        $250
9  OTHER               $0       $12,000      $3,000      $1,000
10 =============================================================
11
12
```

Figure 3.22 The global format for numeric values is specified as Currency with zero decimal places.

to replace the default value, 2. Press ⏎, and the worksheet changes (Fig. 3.22). Every numeric value in the worksheet is now preceded by a dollar sign, and commas are inserted in values where appropriate. Any future numeric values that are entered in the worksheet will also be displayed using Currency format.

The only problem is that the Currency format is not appropriate for the percentages in column B. The Percent or Fixed format is more appropriate for these values.

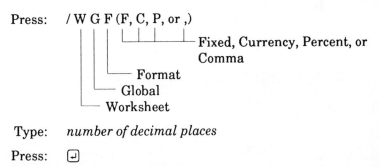

Keystroke Summary: Adjust the format of all numeric values

Press: / W G F (F, C, P, or ,)

            Fixed, Currency, Percent, or Comma

       Format
      Global
     Worksheet

Type: *number of decimal places*

Press: ⏎

Formatting Values in a Given Range

Worksheets frequently require more than one display format for numeric values. When this is the case, the global worksheet format is set to the most common format as described in the previous section. Other formats for specific ranges of the worksheet are then set individually. To illustrate this idea, modify the display format for the budget category percentages to the Percent format.

Position the cell pointer to cell B6. Choose the menu option to define a display format for a given range:

```
/ R F
    └── Format
  └── Range
```

In response to the menu of format choices, press

```
P
└── Percent
```

The prompt

```
Enter number of decimal places (0..15): 2
```

appears. Recall that the Percent format automatically multiplies the internally stored numeric value by 100 before displaying it. Thus it is not necessary to display any decimal places. Type

```
0
```

to replace the suggestion of two decimal places and press ⏎.
    The next prompt,

```
Enter range to format: B6..B6
```

asks you to specify the range of cells that is to use the Percent format. Type

```
B6.B9
```

to overwrite the suggested range address of a single cell. Press ⏎. Note that the percentages are multiplied by 100 and a percent sign is displayed on the right (Fig. 3.23).

```
B6: (P0) [W10] 0.3                                                    READY

          A             B            C          D            E
 1   BUDGET EXPENDITURE BY YEAR AND MONTH
 2   ANNUAL INCOME       $30,000
 3   =================================================================
 4   CATEGORY          PERCENTAGE     ANNUAL   QUARTERLY    MONTHLY
 5   =================================================================
 6   HOUSING                 30%      $9,000     $2,250        $750
 7   FOOD                    20%      $6,000     $1,500        $500
 8   TRANSPORTATION          10%      $3,000       $750        $250
 9   OTHER                   40%     $12,000     $3,000      $1,000
10   =================================================================
11
12
```

Figure 3.23 The range format for the numeric values representing budget category percentages are specified as Percent with zero decimal places. The notation (P0) for cell B6 confirms this range format specification.

Notice the contents of cell B6 as displayed on line 1 of the control panel. The cell contains the numeric value .3, the special column width [W10] for 10 spaces wide, and the special format (P0) for Percent with 0 decimal places. The value .3 is displayed as 30% on the worksheet.

At this point you have successfully modified the worksheet created in Chapter 2 to appear as suggested in Fig. 3.1. However, the chapter tutorial is not complete. In the next section you will learn to modify the worksheet by erasing all or part of it. Save the worksheet on a disk. That way if you make any mistakes erasing the worksheet, you'll be able to recover easily by retrieving it.

Press / F S to choose the menu option to save the worksheet and follow the procedures described in Chapter 2. Use a different file name, MODBUDGT, to indicate that this is a modified budget.

Keystroke Summary: Adjust the format of numeric values in a range

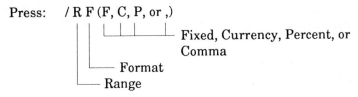

Press: / R F (F, C, P, or ,)
Fixed, Currency, Percent, or Comma
Format
Range

Type: *number of decimal places*

Press: ⏎

Type: *range address*

Press: ⏎

What Can Go Wrong?

1. The display format or number of decimal places is not correct.

Cause: You chose the wrong format option or typed the wrong number of decimal places.

Solution: Redo the procedure from the beginning. Carefully choose the format option and type the number of decimal places desired.

2. You changed the display format of the wrong group of cells.

Cause: You made a mistake in entering the range address.

Solution: Reset the display format of the incorrect group of cells to the default value. Choose the menu options as follows:

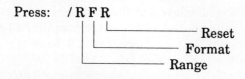

Press: / R F R
Reset
Format
Range

Type: *Range address of incorrect cells*

Press: ↵

Erasing Worksheets

Erasing an Entire Worksheet

Sometimes you'll start a worksheet and simply want to throw away all that you've done and start over. 1-2-3 provides a handy menu feature for doing this. However, be extremely careful because once you have erased a worksheet from the screen, it's gone unless you have already saved it in a disk file.

If you haven't already done so, save the current worksheet in a disk file. Then erase the entire worksheet from the screen by choosing the Erase option from the Worksheet menu:

/ W E
Erase
Worksheet

The following menu appears:

No   Yes

Press Y for Yes, to erase the worksheet, or press N for No, to return to READY mode. Press Y. The contents, column width settings, label-prefixing, and numeric formatting of each cell in the worksheet is erased.

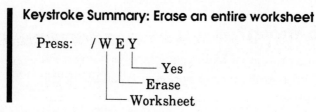

Keystroke Summary: Erase an entire worksheet

Press: / W E Y
Yes
Erase
Worksheet

Erasing a Worksheet Range

More commonly, you'll want to erase only a portion of a worksheet. Earlier in this chapter, you learned to delete columns and rows from a worksheet. This feature allowed you to erase the contents of complete columns and rows and automatically moved succeeding columns and rows to fill in the vacant space. The range erase feature described in this section allows you to erase the contents of all cells in a range address (this may or may not be a complete column or row). This feature does not shift succeeding columns or rows; the erased cells are left blank.

To try this feature, retrieve the modified worksheet (/ F R), MODBUDGT, from disk. Position the cell pointer over cell B4. Choose the menu option to Erase a Range of the worksheet.

```
/ R E
    |
    |---- Erase
    |
    ---- Range
```

You will be prompted to enter the range address you wish to erase:

```
Enter range to erase: B4..B4
```

If you press ⏎, the contents of the highlighted cell, B4, will be erased. Instead, type

B4.D7

to erase the contents of the cells in rows 4 to 7 and columns B to D. Press ⏎, and the range is erased (Fig. 3.24). This erases the contents and label-prefixing of each cell in the designated range. However, column width settings and display format settings remain intact. To see this, position the cell pointer to cell B6. Note that the contents are gone but the column width setting [W10] and display format (P0) are still associated with that cell.

Erasing worksheet ranges is a handy tool for modifying a worksheet, but extreme care must be taken. An error in entering a range address can cause major portions of a worksheet to be lost. A precaution taken by experienced 1-2-3 users is to periodically save the current worksheet in a disk file. Then you can recover from a major error by retrieving the most recently saved version of the worksheet and trying again.

```
B6: (P0) [W10]                                                      READY

        A           B           C           D           E
1  BUDGET EXPENDITURE BY YEAR AND MONTH
2  ANNUAL INCOME      $30,000
3  ================================================================
4  CATEGORY                                              MONTHLY
5  ================                                      ============
6  HOUSING      ████████████                                  $0
7  FOOD                                                        $0
8  TRANSPORTATION      10%     $3,000      $750          $250
9  OTHER               40%    $12,000    $3,000        $1,000
10 ================================================================
11
12
```

Figure 3.24 The contents of all cells in the range address B4..D7 are erased.

This concludes the second 1-2-3 tutorial. There is no need to save the current worksheet, so exit by typing / Q Y.

> **Keystroke Summary: Erase a worksheet range**
>
> Press: / R E
>
> └── Erase
>
> └── Range
>
> Type: *range address*
>
> Press: ↵

Summary

Function	Reference or Keystrokes	Page
Column width, set column	/ W C S, → or ←, ↵	64
Column width, set default	/ W G C, → or ←, ↵	62
Delete columns	/ W D C, range address, ↵	54
Delete rows	/ W D R, range address, ↵	56
Erase range	/ R E, range address, ↵	75
Erase worksheet	/ W E Y	74
Format options	Fixed, Currency, Percent, General, and Comma; Fig.3.21	69
Format, set default	/ W G F, format option, decimal places, ↵	70
Format, set range	/ R F, format option, decimal places, ↵, range address, ↵	72
Insert columns	/ W I C, range address, ↵	59
Insert rows	/ W I R, range address, ↵	61
Label-prefix, set center	/ R L C, range address, ↵	67
Label-prefix, set left	/ R L L, range address, ↵	67
Label-prefix, set right	/ R L R, range address, ↵	67
Range menu options	Fig. 3.19	67
Retrieve file	/ F R, file name, ↵	52
Worksheet menu options	Fig. 3.5	55

Self-Test

1. Indicate the main menu option (Worksheet, Range, or File) that provides options for:

   a. retrieving a file from disk _____

   b. setting the column width of all columns _____

c. setting the display format of a group of cells _____

d. inserting three blank columns _____

2. After pressing / F R to retrieve a file, a list of file names and subdirectory names appear on line 3 of the control panel.

   a. How do you distinguish file names from subdirectory names? _____

   b. How do you select a file name from the list? _____

3. Press _____ to delete the contents of rows 3, 4, and 5 and move the following rows up 3.

4. Cell B8 contains the formula +A8/12. If row 7 is deleted from the worksheet, this formula is automatically converted to _____ and placed in cell B7.

5. Press _____ to insert blank columns in columns B and C and move the current cell contents in these columns two columns to the right.

6. When entering a column width using POINT mode, press _____ to increase the column width 1 unit and press _____ to decrease the column width 1 unit.

7. Press _____ to set the width of all columns in the worksheet from the default of nine spaces to six spaces.

8. Press _____ to align all labels in rows 1 to 5 and columns B to F in the center of the cells.

9. Indicate how each internally stored value will be displayed using the given format in a cell of width 8.

   a. 456.83412, Fixed, 2 decimal places _____

   b. 3561.13, Currency, 0 decimal places _____

   c. 3561.12, Comma, 1 decimal place_____

   d. .78321, Percent, 1 decimal place _____

10. Press _____ to set the display format of all numeric cells in rows 2 to 8 and columns D to F to Fixed format with two decimal places.

11. Press _____ to erase the current worksheet from memory.

12. Press _____ to erase the contents of the currently highlighted cell.

13. Explain the difference between deleting a column using the column delete option in the Worksheet menu group and using the erase option in the Range menu group where the range consists of a single column.

Exercises

1. Print the modified worksheet you created by following the tutorial in this chapter (Fig. 3.1) and submit it to your instructor.

2. Retrieve the college budget worksheet that you created in Chapter 2. Modify it so that it looks like the worksheet illustrated on the next page. Delete any blank columns that you used for spacing. Set column A to 20 spaces and set all other

columns to 12 spaces. Center the column headings ANNUAL, SEMESTER, and MONTH in their respective cells. Use formulas to compute the ANNUAL budget for the OTHER category and for all categories under SEMESTER and MONTH. Print a copy of the completed worksheet.

```
COLLEGE BUDGET
ANNUAL EXPENDITURE      $9,600.00
===============================================================
CATEGORY                 ANNUAL     SEMESTER      MONTH
===============================================================
TUITION                $4,800.00   $2,400.00    $400.00
HOUSING                $3,000.00   $1,500.00    $250.00
BOOKS                    $600.00     $300.00     $50.00
FRATERNITY               $300.00     $150.00     $25.00
CAR                      $300.00     $150.00     $25.00
OTHER                    $600.00     $300.00     $50.00
===============================================================
```

3. Retrieve the batting and slugging average worksheet that you created in Chapter 2. Modify it so that it looks like the worksheet illustrated below. Delete any extra columns that you used for spacing. Set column A to 20 spaces and set all other column widths to 12 spaces. Align the column headings FIRST HALF, SECOND HALF, and TOTAL with the right edge of their respective cells. Use formulas to compute all TOTALS and AVERAGES. Print a copy of the completed worksheet.

```
BATTING AVERAGE COMPUTATION
===============================================================
RESULT               FIRST HALF SECOND HALF       TOTAL
===============================================================
SINGLE                        8           4          12
DOUBLE                        2           2           4
TRIPLE                        2           0           2
HOME RUN                      1           1           2
OUT                          18          23          41
===============================================================
TOTAL AT BATS                31          30          61
===============================================================
BATTING AVERAGE           0.419       0.233       0.328
SLUGGING AVERAGE          0.710       0.400       0.557
```

4

Some Worksheet Shortcuts

This chapter introduces the 1-2-3 features and commands that allow you to:

- use POINT mode to define range addresses
- use POINT mode to define cell addresses in formulas
- copy labels and numbers from one range address to another
- copy formulas from one range address to another
- move cell contents from one range address to another
- use 1-2-3 functions in cell formulas

Overview

In this chapter, you will learn some handy shortcuts for specifying cell addresses and range addresses. Instead of typing a cell or range address, you can use the cursor keys to point to the desired address. This is easier and eliminates many mistakes.

You will also learn about the Copy and Move main menu options. These allow the contents of cells to be copied to other cells or to be moved to other cells. This saves time in creating worksheets. If a number of cells are to contain the same labels, numbers, or formulas, the labels, numbers, or formulas are entered once and "copied" to the other cells. Or, if part of the worksheet needs to be relocated, the cell contents are "moved" all at once to the new location.

Finally, you will learn to use some predefined functions in your formulas. Functions allow formulas to be simpler and perform more complex calculations.

The tutorial continues with the modified budget worksheet that you completed in Chapter 3. You'll begin by using POINT mode to specify range addresses that are to be erased and to specify cell addresses to be used in formulas. Then you will recreate the worksheet using the Copy feature to save time in entering cell information, and you'll use the Move feature to rearrange the worksheet. Finally, you'll use some functions to add information to the worksheet.

Using Point Mode to Enter Addresses

Several times when you were prompted to enter a range address in Chapters 2 and 3, the mode indicator switched to POINT mode. This is to inform you that you can enter the range address by **pointing** to the desired range using the cursor control keys. Rather than pointing, you typed the range address, and the mode indicator changed to EDIT. Typing a range address is generally more difficult and subject to error, but it gave you valuable experience in dealing with range addresses. Now you are ready to learn the easy way—pointing!

Range Addresses

Begin the tutorial by retrieving (/ F R) the worksheet you saved at the end of Chapter 3 (Fig. 4.1). This worksheet is saved under the file name MODBUDGT. In this section, you will learn about POINT mode by erasing parts of this worksheet. Specifically, you'll erase the boundary characters in row 3 and 5 and the formulas in range address C6..E9. Later, you'll restore this information using some shortcut methods.

Begin by erasing the boundary character labels in row 3 (range address A3..E3). Position the cell pointer on cell A3 and press

to choose the menu option to erase a range of the worksheet (Fig. 4.2). You are prompted to enter the range address to be erased. Since you positioned

```
        A              B          C          D          E
1  BUDGET EXPENDITURE BY YEAR AND MONTH
2  ANNUAL INCOME      $30,000
3  =======================================================================
4  CATEGORY           PERCENTAGE    ANNUAL   QUARTERLY    MONTHLY
5  =======================================================================
6  HOUSING                30%       $9,000     $2,250       $750
7  FOOD                   20%       $6,000     $1,500       $500
8  TRANSPORTATION         10%       $3,000       $750       $250
9  OTHER                  40%      $12,000     $3,000     $1,000
10 =======================================================================
11
12
```

Figure 4.1 The tutorial begins with the MODBUDGT worksheet created in Chapter 3.

the cell pointer on A3, the range A3..A3 is automatically selected. The mode indicator is set to POINT.

In Chapter 3 you were instructed to type the range address to be erased; in this chapter you will use the cursor keys to point to it. Press ⊡. The range address changes to A3..B3, and the corresponding cells are highlighted. Press ⊡ three more times, and the range address A3..E3 will be highlighted and entered at the prompt (Fig. 4.3). Press ⏎ to accept the currently displayed range address, and the equals sign labels used to divide the table will be erased.

Enter range to erase: A3..A3

```
        A              B          C          D          E
1  BUDGET EXPENDITURE BY YEAR AND MONTH
2  ANNUAL INCOME      $30,000
3  ================
4  CATEGORY           PERCENTAGE    ANNUAL   QUARTERLY    MONTHLY
5  =======================================================================
6  HOUSING                30%       $9,000     $2,250       $750
7  FOOD                   20%       $6,000     $1,500       $500
8  TRANSPORTATION         10%       $3,000       $750       $250
9  OTHER                  40%      $12,000     $3,000     $1,000
10 =======================================================================
11
12
```

Figure 4.2 After choosing the menu options / R E, you are prompted to point to the range address to be erased. Range address A3..A3 is automatically filled in and highlighted, since the cell pointer is on cell A3.

Some Worksheet Shortcuts   81
Using Point Mode to Enter Addresses

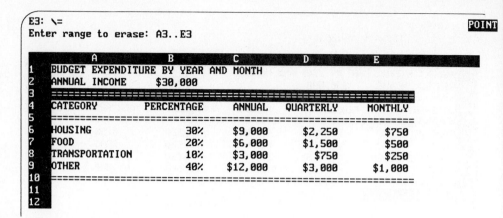

Figure 4.3 The worksheet looks like this after you press ⊡ four times to point to the range of cells to be erased. Press ⏎, and the highlighted cells will be erased.

Notice that instead of typing the range address as in previous chapters, you are pointing to it. The cell highlighting gives you visual information that you are specifying the correct range. This reduces the chance of making a mistake in specifying a range address.

Notice also that as you pointed to the range address, the first cell (A3) in the address was fixed. In many cases the cell highlighted by the cell pointer is automatically specified as a corner of the range. This initial corner is called an **anchor cell**. The cursor keys allow you to expand the range address from the anchor cell to the opposite corner. The automatic specification of the anchor cell is overcome by pressing (Esc) when you are prompted to point to the range address.

To illustrate the anchor cell concept, position the cell pointer on cell A1 and try to erase row 5 (range address A5..E5). Press / R E to select the range erase menu option. You'll be prompted to point to the range address starting with A1..A1. Press ⬇ to highlight the range in row 5. This is impossible because the range is automatically anchored with a corner in cell A1.

To free the anchor cell, press

(Esc)

Now press ⬇ four times to highlight cell A5. Notice that each time you press ⬇, the beginning cell of the range address (or anchor cell) changes. Press

. (period)

to fix the anchor cell as A5 (Fig. 4.4). Complete the erasure of row 5 by pressing ⊡ four times to highlight the desired range. Press ⏎. Row 5 will be erased, and you will return to READY mode.

Generally, in using a command that asks you to point to a range address, it is easier to highlight a corner of the range address before you start. This

```
A5: [W16] \=                                                    POINT
Enter range to erase: A5..A5
```

	A	B	C	D	E
1	BUDGET EXPENDITURE BY YEAR AND MONTH				
2	ANNUAL INCOME	$30,000			
3					
4	CATEGORY	PERCENTAGE	ANNUAL	QUARTERLY	MONTHLY
5	=================	===			
6	HOUSING	30%	$9,000	$2,250	$750
7	FOOD	20%	$6,000	$1,500	$500
8	TRANSPORTATION	10%	$3,000	$750	$250
9	OTHER	40%	$12,000	$3,000	$1,000
10	==				
11					
12					

Figure 4.4 The cell pointer initially highlighted cell A1. This became the anchor cell of the range address. After you press (Esc), the anchor cell is released. A5 becomes the new anchor cell after you highlight it and press . (period).

becomes the anchor cell, and you only need to point to an opposite corner of the range address. But if you forget, simply press (Esc), and you may choose any cell as the anchor cell.

For additional practice and to prepare for the tutorial exercises later in this chapter, erase the formulas in cells C6..E9. Point to this range address in reverse order. Position the cell pointer on E9, the lower right corner of the range. Press / R E to choose the Range Erase menu option. E9 is the anchor cell. Press ⊟ twice and ⊤ three times to specify the range address E9..C6 (Fig. 4.5). Press ⏎ to erase.

```
C6: +B2*B6                                                      POINT
Enter range to erase: E9..C6
```

	A	B	C	D	E
1	BUDGET EXPENDITURE BY YEAR AND MONTH				
2	ANNUAL INCOME	$30,000			
3					
4	CATEGORY	PERCENTAGE	ANNUAL	QUARTERLY	MONTHLY
5					
6	HOUSING	30%	$9,000	$2,250	$750
7	FOOD	20%	$6,000	$1,500	$500
8	TRANSPORTATION	10%	$3,000	$750	$250
9	OTHER	40%	$12,000	$3,000	$1,000
10	==				
11					
12					

Figure 4.5 The cell pointer is initially on cell E9. You used ⊟ and ⊤ to highlight the range address E9..C6. Press ⏎, and the highlighted cells will be erased.

Press: ⊟, ⊡, ⬆, or ⬇ to highlight a corner (or anchor) cell

Press: . (period)

Press: ⊟, ⊡, ⬆, or ⬇ to specify an opposite corner and high-
          light the range of cells

Press: ↵

Note: In some cases the cell containing the cell pointer is
          automatically defined as the anchor cell, and you skip
          Steps 1 and 2.

Cell Addresses

Pointing can also be used to reduce errors in typing cell addresses in formulas. For example, the formula entered in cell C6 (before you erased it) was
+B2*B6. This formula can be entered by typing as you did in Chapter 2 or by
pointing first to cell B2 and then to cell B6. Continue the tutorial by reentering this formula.

Position the cell pointer over cell C6. Type + to begin the formula, and the
mode indicator changes to VALUE. Instead of typing the cell address, B2,
press ⊟ once and press ⬆ four times to position the cell pointer over B2 (Fig.
4.6). Notice that as soon as you press a cursor key, the mode indicator
changes to POINT mode. Also notice that with each press of a cursor key, the
address of the currently highlighted cell is inserted in the formula.

Once you have highlighted cell B2, continue the formula by typing an
asterisk, the multiplication operator. The cell pointer returns to cell C6, and
the mode indicator returns to VALUE (Fig. 4.7). The formula continues with

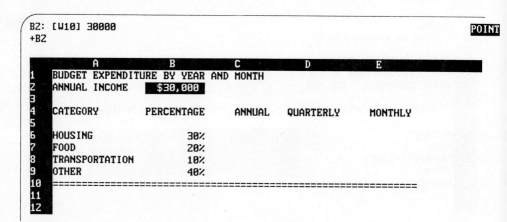

Figure 4.6 After beginnning the formula for cell C6 with a plus sign, press ⊟ once
and ⬆ four times to point to cell B2. Each time a new cell is highlighted, the cell
address is inserted in the formula.

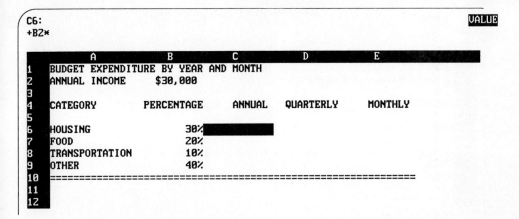

```
C6:                                                              VALUE
+B2*

            A          B          C        D          E
1   BUDGET EXPENDITURE BY YEAR AND MONTH
2   ANNUAL INCOME     $30,000
3
4   CATEGORY          PERCENTAGE    ANNUAL  QUARTERLY    MONTHLY
5
6   HOUSING              30%████████████
7   FOOD                 20%
8   TRANSPORTATION       10%
9   OTHER                40%
10  ==========================================================
11
12
```

Figure 4.7 After you type the multiplication operator (asterisk), the cell pointer returns to cell C6, the mode indicator returns to VALUE, and you may continue entering the formula.

another cell address. Press ⊟ once to highlight cell B6. The mode indicator returns to POINT mode, and the cell address B6 is inserted in your formula. Press ⏎ to complete the formula. The cell pointer returns to C6, the formula is entered in the cell, and the mode indicator changes to READY (Fig. 4.8).

When you are pointing to a cell address in a formula, there are two ways to complete the pointing process. One is to type a formula operator such as an arithmetic sign (+, −, *, or /) or a parenthesis; this is appropriate when the formula is not complete and you wish to continue. The other way to complete the pointing process is to press ⏎. This completes the formula and enters it in the worksheet cell.

```
C6:  +B2*B6                                                     READY

            A          B          C        D          E
1   BUDGET EXPENDITURE BY YEAR AND MONTH
2   ANNUAL INCOME     $30,000
3
4   CATEGORY          PERCENTAGE    ANNUAL  QUARTERLY    MONTHLY
5
6   HOUSING              30%     $9,000
7   FOOD                 20%
8   TRANSPORTATION       10%
9   OTHER                40%
10  ==========================================================
11
12
```

Figure 4.8 Continue the formula for cell C6 by pointing to cell B6 to insert this cell address in the formula. Pressing ⏎ completes the formula and returns you to READY mode as illustrated.

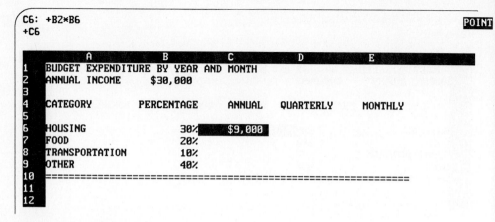

```
C6: +B2×B6                                                    POINT
+C6

        A              B            C          D          E
1  BUDGET EXPENDITURE BY YEAR AND MONTH
2  ANNUAL INCOME        $30,000
3
4  CATEGORY          PERCENTAGE    ANNUAL    QUARTERLY    MONTHLY
5
6  HOUSING              30%        $9,000
7  FOOD                 20%
8  TRANSPORTATION       10%
9  OTHER                40%
10 ==================================================================
11
12
```

Figure 4.9 After beginning the formula for cell D6 with a plus sign, press ⊟ once to point to cell C6. This cell address is entered in the formula when you continue by pressing the division operator, /.

For practice, enter the formula +C6/4 in cell D6. Position the cell pointer over D6 and type +. Press ⊟ once to point to cell C6 (Fig. 4.9). Type the division operator, /, to complete the pointing process. Complete the formula by typing the divisor, 4, and pressing ⏎. Use a similar procedure to enter the formula +C6/12 in cell E6 (Fig. 4.10).

Keystroke Summary: Point to a cell address

Press: ⬅, ➡, ⬆, or ⬇ to highlight the desired cell address

Press: ⏎ or a formula operator (for example: +, –,), (, *, or /) to place the cell address in the formula and return the cell pointer to the formula cell

```
E6: +C6/12                                                   READY

        A              B            C          D          E
1  BUDGET EXPENDITURE BY YEAR AND MONTH
2  ANNUAL INCOME        $30,000
3
4  CATEGORY          PERCENTAGE    ANNUAL    QUARTERLY    MONTHLY
5
6  HOUSING              30%        $9,000    $2,250        $750
7  FOOD                 20%
8  TRANSPORTATION       10%
9  OTHER                40%
10 ==================================================================
11
12
```

Figure 4.10 After you have reentered the formulas for ANNUAL, QUARTERLY, and MONTHLY HOUSING expense, the worksheet looks like this.

What Can Go Wrong?

1. While typing a formula, you entered POINT mode and a cell address was inserted at the wrong place in the formula.

Cause: You pressed a cursor movement key while typing the formula.

Solution: Press Esc. This erases the address from the formula, returns the cell pointer to the formula cell, and returns the mode indicator to VALUE.

2. The formula is entered in the worksheet and you are returned to READY mode before the formula was complete.

Cause: You pressed ↵ before the formula was complete. Remember that you may leave POINT mode by entering an arithmetic operator to continue the formula.

Solution: Position the cell pointer over the cell with the incomplete formula. Either reenter the formula from the beginning or press F2 to edit the formula.

Copying Data from One Part of the Worksheet to Another

One of the handiest features 1-2-3 provides for quickly entering cell data is the Copy menu option. Press / and highlight the Copy option as illustrated in Fig. 4.11. This option allows you to **copy** the contents of a cell or range of cells to another location in the worksheet. This is a useful feature if you plan to enter a lot of repetitive information in a worksheet. For example, in the tutorial worksheet, 15 cells contain the label \=. By using the Copy feature, this label is entered once and copied to the remaining cells. Also, similar formulas are used in the tutorial worksheet to calculate the ANNUAL, QUARTERLY, and MONTHLY expenditure in each category. These too can be entered once and copied to the corresponding cells in the remaining categories. Note also the Move menu option. This is similar to the Copy option and is discussed in the next section.

```
E6:  +C6/12                                                          MENU
Worksheet  Range  Copy  Move  File  Print  Graph  Data  System  Add-In  Quit
Copy a cell or range of cells
```

Figure 4.11 Use the Copy menu option to copy the contents of cells in one range to cells in another range.

The discussion of the Copy feature is divided into two parts: copying labels and numbers and copying formulas. Copying labels and numbers is straightforward; an exact duplicate of the label or number is copied from one cell to another. Copying formulas is more complex, since the cell addresses in the formulas may or may not be adjusted during the copy operation.

Copying Labels or Numbers

To illustrate the copy feature, you'll reenter the labels \= in rows 3 and 5 of the worksheet. The label is entered once in cell A3 and copied to the remaining cells in row 3 (range address: B3..E3). A second copy operation copies the labels in row 3 to the cells in row 5.

Press Esc to exit the menu system. Position the cell pointer on A3 and type the label

    \=

Press ⏎ to restore the label in cell A3.

Copy this label to the remaining cells in row 3. Leave the cell pointer on A3 and press

    / C
      └─ Copy

to select the Copy option from the menu. First, you'll be prompted to enter the range address to copy FROM (Fig. 4.12). Range address A3..A3 is automatically filled in, and A3 is fixed as the anchor cell. You're in POINT mode.

```
A3: [W16] \=                                                    POINT
Enter range to copy FROM: A3..A3

            A          B          C         D          E
1   BUDGET EXPENDITURE BY YEAR AND MONTH
2   ANNUAL INCOME      $30,000
3   ===============
4   CATEGORY        PERCENTAGE    ANNUAL   QUARTERLY   MONTHLY
5
6   HOUSING              30%      $9,000    $2,250      $750
7   FOOD                 20%
8   TRANSPORTATION       10%
9   OTHER                40%
10  ============================================================
11
12
```

Figure 4.12 Specify the range address A3..A3 to copy the label \= from the single cell A3 to another range of the worksheet. The cell pointer position is automatically defined as the anchor cell of the copy FROM range.

Since you wish to copy only the label from this single cell, press ⏎ to accept the range address given.

Next, you'll be prompted to enter the range address to copy TO. You're in POINT mode, and there is no anchor cell fixed. Press → once to highlight cell B3. Press . (period) to fix B3 as the anchor cell, and press → three more times to highlight the range address B3..E3 (Fig. 4.13). Complete the copy operation by pressing ⏎. The label in the copy FROM range, A3..A3, is copied to all of the cells in the copy TO range, B3..E3.

There are a few considerations in using the copy feature. First, the copy FROM range does not have to contain the same number of cells as the copy TO range. In your example the copy FROM range contains one cell and the copy TO range contains four cells. Second, if the range addresses in the TO and FROM range contain the same number of cells, it is necessary to specify only the upper left corner of the TO range. This is illustrated below. Third, the range addresses may be typed rather than pointed to, though pointing seems easier and less prone to error.

For further practice, copy the labels in row 3 into row 5. Position the cell pointer on cell A3 and press / C to choose the Copy menu feature. In response to the prompt to enter the range to copy FROM, press → four times to point to the range A3..E3 (Fig. 4.14). Press ⏎, and the cell pointer returns to cell A3.

Next, enter the range to copy TO. Recall that the anchor cell is not fixed for the copy TO range. Press ↓ twice to point to cell A5 (the upper left corner of the copy TO range) as illustrated in Fig. 4.15. Since the copy FROM and copy TO range addresses contain the same number of cells, it is necessary to

```
E3:                                                              POINT
Enter range to copy TO: B3..E3

          A              B              C          D              E
1   BUDGET EXPENDITURE BY YEAR AND MONTH
2   ANNUAL INCOME        $30,000
3   ================
4   CATEGORY            PERCENTAGE     ANNUAL     QUARTERLY      MONTHLY
5
6   HOUSING                  30%       $9,000      $2,250         $750
7   FOOD                     20%
8   TRANSPORTATION           10%
9   OTHER                    40%
10  ==================================================================
11
12
```

Figure 4.13 Specify the range address B3..E3 to receive duplicate copies of the label contained in cell A3. It is necessary to specify an anchor cell, by positioning the cell pointer and typing a . (period), for the copy TO range.

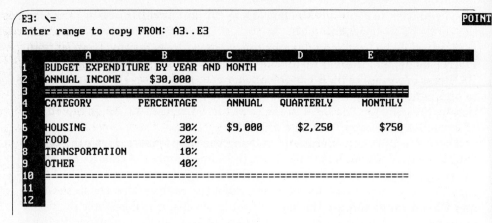

Figure 4.14 Specify the range address A3..E3 to copy the divider labels in the cells of row 3 to another range of the worksheet.

specify only the upper left corner of the copy TO range. Press ⏎ to complete the copy operation.

Copying Formulas

In copying labels and numbers, an exact copy of the contents of cells in the copy FROM range is made to the cells in the copy TO range. This is not the case in copying formulas. The manner in which formulas are copied depends on the way cell addresses in the formula are specified. Cell addresses may be specified as **relative** or **absolute**. So far, all of the formulas in the sample worksheet have been written using relative cell addresses.

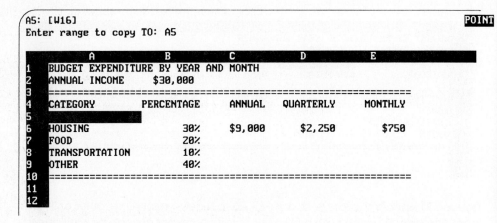

Figure 4.15 Specify the upper left corner of the range address to receive a copy of the divider labels from row 3. Press ⏎ to complete the copy operation.

```
         A          B           C          D           E
1  BUDGET EXPENDITURE BY YEAR AND MONTH
2  ANNUAL INCOME      $30,000
3  ==================================================================
4  CATEGORY        PERCENTAGE    ANNUAL    QUARTERLY    MONTHLY
5  ==================================================================
6  HOUSING             30%      $9,000      $2,250       $750
7  FOOD                20%                     $0         $0
8  TRANSPORTATION      10%                     $0         $0
9  OTHER               40%                     $0         $0
10 ==================================================================
11
12
```

Figure 4.16 After you have copied the formulas in range address D6..E6 to D7..E9, the worksheet looks like this.

To understand the idea of a relative cell address, continue the tutorial by copying the formulas in range D6..E6 to the range D7..E9. Position the cell pointer on cell D6. Press / C to select the Copy menu option. Press ⊡ once to select the copy FROM range D6..E6 and press ⏎. The cell pointer will return to cell D6. Now press ⊡ to position the cell pointer on cell D7, and press . (period) to fix the anchor cell of the copy TO range. Press ⊡ once and ⊡ twice to select the copy TO range D7..E9. Press ⏎ to complete the copy operation (Fig. 4.16).

The formula in cell D6, +C6/4 is copied to cells D7, D8, and D9. Position the cell pointer on D7 (Fig. 4.17). Take a careful look at the copied formula,

```
         A          B           C          D           E
1  BUDGET EXPENDITURE BY YEAR AND MONTH
2  ANNUAL INCOME      $30,000
3  ==================================================================
4  CATEGORY        PERCENTAGE    ANNUAL    QUARTERLY    MONTHLY
5  ==================================================================
6  HOUSING             30%      $9,000      $2,250       $750
7  FOOD                20%                     $0         $0
8  TRANSPORTATION      10%                     $0         $0
9  OTHER               40%                     $0         $0
10 ==================================================================
11
12
```

Figure 4.17 The formula in cell D6, +C6/4, involves a relative cell address. The formula takes the contents of the cell one column to the left and divides by 4. When copied to cell D7, the formula becomes +C7/4, since C7 is the cell one column to the left of D7.

Some Worksheet Shortcuts   **91**
Copying Data from One Part of the Worksheet
to Another

+C7/4. The cell address in the copied formula is adjusted so that it represents the same relative position to the cell being copied TO. That is, the formula in D6 specifies a relative cell location. It says to take the value in the cell one column to the left and divide it by 4. Therefore, when copied to cell D7, the formula is adjusted so that cell C7, which is one column to the left of D7, is divided by 4.

Likewise, the formulas in cells D8 and D9 are copied so that the cell one column to the left is divided by 4. Position the cell pointer on each of these cells and verify that each formula references the same relative cell location. All of these cells contain the value $0 because the cell one column to the left has no value at this time.

Similarly, the formula in cell E6, +C6/12, is copied to cells E7, E8, and E9 by adjusting the cell reference C6 so that it represents the same relative cell location to the cell being copied TO. That is, the value in E6 is computed by taking the value in the cell two columns to the left and dividing by 12. A similar formula appears in cells E7, E8, and E9. Position the cell pointer on each of these cells and verify that the formula contained in each represents the same relative calculation.

Position the cell pointer to cell C6. The formula is +B2*B6. In relative terms, the formula says to take the value in the cell one column to the left and four rows up and multiply it by the value in the cell one column to the left. If this formula is copied to cell C7 and adjusted to represent the same relative calculation, it becomes +B3*B7. This is not what is wanted, since cell B3 contains the label \=, rather than the annual income figure. Clearly, in some cases, copying the relative position of cells is useful, and in some cases it is not.

Ideally, to copy the formula +B2*B6 to cell C7, you want B2 to be copied exactly and B6 to be copied by using the same relative position. This can be accomplished by declaring that B2 is an absolute cell address and that B6 is a relative cell address.

As you know, a cell address is composed of a column letter followed by a row number, for example, B2. This is treated as a relative cell address in copying a formula. If the column letter and the row number are each preceded by a $ sign, the cell address is treated as an absolute cell address in copying a formula. For example, $B$2 refers to cell location B2 but specifies that during a copy operation this cell address is to be treated as an absolute cell address and copied exactly.

Therefore to copy the formula in cell C6 to cells C7, C8, and C9 appropriately, the formula in cell C6 needs to be adjusted to read +$B$2*B6. That way, when the formula is copied, the cell address $B$2 is copied exactly, and the cell address B6 is adjusted to the correct relative position.

Edit the formula in cell C6. Position the cell pointer to cell C6 and press

F2

Press ⊡ so that the cursor is positioned anywhere under the cell address B2 in the formula. The additional $ signs can be typed, but 1-2-3 provides a

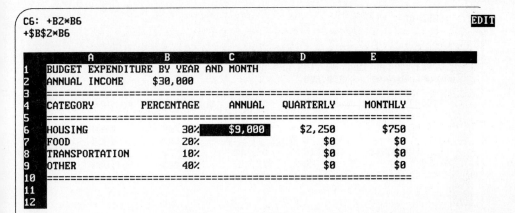

```
C6: +B2*B6                                                      EDIT
+$B$2*B6

          A             B            C           D           E
1   BUDGET EXPENDITURE BY YEAR AND MONTH
2   ANNUAL INCOME       $30,000
3   ============================================================
4   CATEGORY          PERCENTAGE     ANNUAL    QUARTERLY    MONTHLY
5   ============================================================
6   HOUSING                30%       $9,000      $2,250       $750
7   FOOD                   20%                      $0         $0
8   TRANSPORTATION         10%                      $0         $0
9   OTHER                  40%                      $0         $0
10  ============================================================
11
12
```

Figure 4.18 Convert the cell address B2 to an absolute cell address $B$2 by editing the contents of C6. Move the edit cursor under cell B2 and press F4. The $ signs are inserted ahead of the column letter and row number.

function key to make a cell address absolute. This key can be used in EDIT mode as you are doing here or in POINT mode when you are pointing to a cell address. Press

F4

to convert the cell address B2 to $B$2 (Fig. 4.18). Press ↵, and the revised formula is entered in cell C6.

Notice that converting this cell address from relative to absolute has no effect on the computation of the budgeted annual housing expenditure. The only reason you made the conversion is to use the Copy command to copy this formula to the other cells. However, the Copy command is so useful that you will want to design your formulas so that they may be easily and correctly copied.

Finally, you are ready to copy this formula to range address C7..C9. The cell pointer is positioned on cell C6. Press / C to choose the Copy menu option. Press ↵ to accept the copy FROM range C6..C6. Press ↓ and . (period) to choose anchor cell C7 for the copy TO range. Press ↓ two times, and press ↵ to complete the copy operation.

Now that the annual expenditure in each category is computed, the quarterly and monthly expenditures are filled in. Position the cell pointer on cell C7 (Fig. 4.19) and study the copied formula, +$B$2*B7. The absolute cell reference ($B$2) in cell C6 is copied exactly, and the relative cell reference (B6) is adjusted to B7, the cell to the immediate left.

The Copy menu option is a 1-2-3 feature that is used over and over to create and modify worksheets quickly. The key to using this feature to copy formulas is to understand the appropriate use of the absolute and relative cell references.

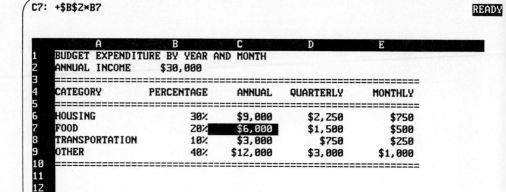

Figure 4.19 The formula in cell C6, +$B$2*B6, involves both an absolute cell address and a relative cell address. The formula takes the contents of absolute cell address B2 times the contents of the cell one column to the left. When copied to cell C7, the formula becomes +$B$2*B7. The absolute cell address is copied exactly, and the relative address is one column to the left of C7.

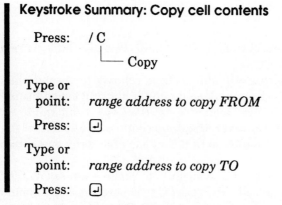

Keystroke Summary: Copy cell contents

Press: / C
              └── Copy

Type or
   point: *range address to copy FROM*

Press: ⏎

Type or
   point: *range address to copy TO*

Press: ⏎

What Can Go Wrong?

1. You successfully pointed to the copy FROM range address, but when pointing to the copy TO range address, the cell pointer doesn't stay in one place, so you can highlight the correct range.

Cause: The copy FROM range address is automatically anchored using the cell address to which you pointed at the beginning of the copy operation. You must anchor the copy TO range address yourself.

Solution: Position the cell pointer at one corner of the copy TO range address. Press . (period) to fix this cell as an anchor. Now point to the desired range and press ⏎.

2. You are editing the formula in cell C6 to make the reference to cell B2 an absolute address. The cell address is changed to B$2 or $B2 rather than $B$2 as expected.

Cause: You pressed F4 more than once. Each time F4 is pressed, the cell address changes among the forms: B2, $B$2, B$2, and $B2. The two unfamiliar forms are called mixed cell addresses.

Solution: With the EDIT cursor positioned under B2, continue to press F4 until the desired cell address is displayed. Press ⏎.

3. After one of the copy operations, the worksheet is not as shown in the illustrations.

Cause: You incorrectly specified the copy FROM or copy TO range address. These range addresses should never overlap.

Solution: If there is not much damage, edit the contents of the incorrect cells by positioning the cell pointer and pressing F2. Otherwise, retrieve the file MODBUDGT and redo the tutorial.

Moving Data from One Part of the Worksheet to Another

Move is a main menu option to **move** the contents of cells from a given range to cells in another range. The cells in the move FROM range are erased after the contents are moved. This is almost identical to the Copy menu option, except that with the Copy option, the cell contents of the FROM range are left as before rather than being erased. Copy is useful for duplicating cell labels, numbers, and formulas; Move is useful for rearranging the cells in a worksheet.

To illustrate the Move option, you'll continue the tutorial by rearranging the ANNUAL, QUARTERLY, and MONTHLY columns so that the MONTHLY column is first and the ANNUAL column is last. Begin by moving the ANNUAL column to column F of the worksheet.

Position the cell pointer on cell C3. Press

/ M
└─ Move

to choose the Move menu option. You will be prompted to enter the range of cells to move FROM. Press ⬇ seven times to highlight the range address C3..C10 (Fig. 4.20). Press ⏎ to accept the move FROM range.

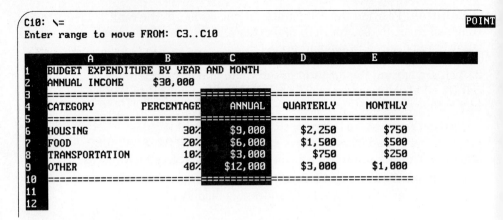

```
C10: \=
Enter range to move FROM: C3..C10                              POINT

        A          B          C         D          E
1   BUDGET EXPENDITURE BY YEAR AND MONTH
2   ANNUAL INCOME      $30,000
3   ==========================================================
4   CATEGORY       PERCENTAGE    ANNUAL    QUARTERLY    MONTHLY
5   ==========================================================
6   HOUSING            30%       $9,000      $2,250       $750
7   FOOD               20%       $6,000      $1,500       $500
8   TRANSPORTATION     10%       $3,000        $750       $250
9   OTHER              40%      $12,000      $3,000     $1,000
10  ==========================================================
11
12
```

Figure 4.20 Specify the range address C3..C10 to move the contents of the cells in the ANNUAL column to another location on the worksheet.

Next, you'll be prompted to enter the move TO range. Press ⊟ three times to specify F3 as the anchor cell of the move TO range (Fig. 4.21). As with the Copy command, it is enough to specify the upper left corner of the TO range. Press ⏎ to accept F3 as the upper left corner of the TO range.

The worksheet now appears as in Fig. 4.22. The contents of the move FROM range, C3..C10, are erased, and the labels, numbers, and formulas are moved to the move TO range, F3..F10. Move the cell pointer to column F and verify that the move has taken place.

```
F3:                                                            POINT
Enter range to move TO: F3

        B          C         D          E         F          G
1   RE BY YEAR AND MONTH
2      $30,000
3   ===================================================
4   PERCENTAGE    ANNUAL   QUARTERLY    MONTHLY
5   ===================================================
6       30%       $9,000    $2,250        $750
7       20%       $6,000    $1,500        $500
8       10%       $3,000      $750        $250
9       40%      $12,000    $3,000      $1,000
10  ===================================================
11
12
```

Figure 4.21 Specify the range address to receive the column of ANNUAL budget expenditures. It is enough to specify the upper left corner of the range.

96

	A	B	C	D	E
1	BUDGET EXPENDITURE BY YEAR AND MONTH				
2	ANNUAL INCOME	$30,000			
3	=========================			=============================	
4	CATEGORY	PERCENTAGE		QUARTERLY	MONTHLY
5	=========================			=============================	
6	HOUSING	30%		$2,250	$750
7	FOOD	20%		$1,500	$500
8	TRANSPORTATION	10%		$750	$250
9	OTHER	40%		$3,000	$1,000
10	=========================			=============================	
11					
12					

Figure 4.22 After the contents of the cells in the range C3..C10 are moved to column F of the worksheet, the cells in this range are erased.

Continue rearranging the columns by moving the MONTHLY column to column C. Position the cell pointer on cell E3. Press / M to select the Move menu option. Press ⬇ seven times to highlight the move FROM range E3..E10, and press ⏎. Press ⬅ two times to highlight cell C3, the upper left corner of the move TO range, and press ⏎. The contents of the cells in the MONTHLY column are moved to column C (Fig. 4.23).

The rearrangement can be completed by either moving the ANNUAL column (now in column F) to column E or deleting column E. Use the latter

	A	B	C	D	E
1	BUDGET EXPENDITURE BY YEAR AND MONTH				
2	ANNUAL INCOME	$30,000			
3	==				
4	CATEGORY	PERCENTAGE	MONTHLY	QUARTERLY	
5	==				
6	HOUSING	30%	$750	$2,250	
7	FOOD	20%	$500	$1,500	
8	TRANSPORTATION	10%	$250	$750	
9	OTHER	40%	$1,000	$3,000	
10	==				
11					
12					

Figure 4.23 The cell contents of range address E3..E10 are moved to column C of the worksheet.

Some Worksheet Shortcuts   97
Moving Data from One Part of the Worksheet
to Another

	A	B	C	D	E
1	BUDGET EXPENDITURE BY YEAR AND MONTH				
2	ANNUAL INCOME	$30,000			
3	===				
4	CATEGORY	PERCENTAGE	MONTHLY	QUARTERLY	ANNUAL
5	===				
6	HOUSING	30%	$750	$2,250	$9,000
7	FOOD	20%	$500	$1,500	$6,000
8	TRANSPORTATION	10%	$250	$750	$3,000
9	OTHER	40%	$1,000	$3,000	$12,000
10	===				
11					
12					

Figure 4.24 After you have deleted column E from the worksheet, Column F, containing the ANNUAL budget amount, moves over to fill in the vacant column. This completes the rearrangement of the worksheet columns.

approach, which you learned in Chapter 3. Position the cell pointer on any cell in column E and press / W D C to delete a column from the worksheet. Press ⏎ in response to the prompt to enter the range of columns to delete (Fig. 4.24).

The Move menu option is extremely useful in rearranging a worksheet. All formulas in the worksheet are automatically adjusted as appropriate. For example, notice the formulas in cells E6, D6, and C6, as given below:

       E6: +$B$2*B6
       D6: +E6/4
       C6: +E6/12

The formula in cell E6 is identical to the formula that used to be in cell C6, since the cells referenced are in the same location. The formulas in cells D6 and C6 are based on the ANNUAL budget expenditure and are updated to reflect the fact that the ANNUAL budget expenditure is now in column E.

Keystroke Summary: Move cell contents

Press: / M
            └── Move

Type or
point: *range address to move FROM*

Press: ⏎

Type or
point: *range address to move TO*

Press: ⏎

Functions

1-2-3 provides an extensive library of predefined procedures to perform certain calculations. These are called **functions** and are generally used in formulas. To illustrate the use of functions, you'll modify the tutorial worksheet to include a row of column totals in row 11.

Position the cell pointer on cell A11. Type the label

TOTAL

and press ⏎. Now position the cell pointer on cell C11 and consider entering a formula to total the monthly expenditures in each budget category. You could enter the formula +C6+C7+C8+C9. However, 1-2-3 provides a function called @SUM to simplify this formula.

All 1-2-3 functions begin with the @ sign and have a name that suggests the computation performed. @SUM is a function to sum the values in a list of cell range addresses. The form of the @SUM function listed in the 1-2-3 manual is

@SUM(list)

SUM is the name of the function, and list is the argument of the function. "List" is a term used in the 1-2-3 manual to refer to one or more range addresses. This function may be used in a cell formula. For example, the following formulas using @SUM are interpreted as follows:

Formula	Means
@SUM(C6..C9)	add the values in cells C6, C7, C8, and C9
@SUM(C6..C7,C8..C9)	same as above but the list contains two range addresses
@SUM(C6..C9)/2	same as above except the sum is divided by 2

Now enter the formula in cell C11. Type

@SUM(

and point to the range address. Press ⬆ five times to point to cell C6. Press . (period) to fix the anchor cell, and press ⬇ three times to highlight the range address C6..C9. Type

)

to complete the function, and press ⏎ to complete the formula (Fig. 4.25).

1-2-3 provides mathematical functions, logical functions, specialized cell functions, string functions, date and time functions, financial functions, and statistical functions. Some of the most commonly used functions are the statistical functions listed in Fig. 4.26. All of these functions require a list of range addresses as an argument and return a single computed value from the values in the cells of the listed ranges.

```
C11:  @SUM(C6..C9)                                                    READY
```

	A	B	C	D	E
1	BUDGET EXPENDITURE BY YEAR AND MONTH				
2	ANNUAL INCOME	$30,000			
3	=======	=======	=======	=======	=======
4	CATEGORY	PERCENTAGE	MONTHLY	QUARTERLY	ANNUAL
5	=======	=======	=======	=======	=======
6	HOUSING	30%	$750	$2,250	$9,000
7	FOOD	20%	$500	$1,500	$6,000
8	TRANSPORTATION	10%	$250	$750	$3,000
9	OTHER	40%	$1,000	$3,000	$12,000
10	=======	=======	=======	=======	=======
11	TOTAL		$2,500		
12					

Figure 4.25 Use the built-in function @SUM(C6..C9) to add the MONTHLY budget expenditures.

Some functions require more than one argument. For example, the function @PMT computes the periodic payment required to pay back a sum of borrowed money. The form of the @PMT function listed in the 1-2-3 manual is,

@PMT(prin,int,term)

This function requires three arguments: the initial amount of the loan (prin), the interest rate per period (int), and the number of payments required to pay back the loan (term). Each of these arguments is a single numeric value that may be entered directly or indirectly by referencing a cell containing the desired value.

Function	Calculates
@AVG(list)	the average value of all cells in the list
@COUNT(list)	the number of nonblank cells in the list
@MAX(list)	the largest value of all cells in the list
@MIN(list)	the smallest value of all cells in the list
@STD(list)	the standard deviation of the values of the cells in the list
@SUM(list)	the total value of all cells in the list
@VAR(list)	the variance of the values of the cells in the list

Figure 4.26 These statistical functions are commonly used in 1-2-3 formulas. *Note:* "List" refers to a list of range addresses separated by commas.

	A	B	C	D	E
1	BUDGET EXPENDITURE BY YEAR AND MONTH				
2	ANNUAL INCOME	$30,000		PAYMENT	$1,498
3	=====	=====	=====	=====	=====
4	CATEGORY	PERCENTAGE	MONTHLY	QUARTERLY	ANNUAL
5	=====	=====	=====	=====	=====
6	HOUSING	30%	$750	$2,250	$9,000
7	FOOD	20%	$500	$1,500	$6,000
8	TRANSPORTATION	10%	$250	$750	$3,000
9	OTHER	40%	$1,000	$3,000	$12,000
10	=====	=====	=====	=====	=====
11	TOTAL		$2,500		
12					

Figure 4.27 Use the built-in function @PMT(B2,.015,24) to calculate the monthly payment required to pay back a $30,000 loan (cell B2) at an interest rate of 0.015 per month, over a 24-month period.

Suppose the $30,000 annual income in the tutorial example is to be borrowed for 24 months at an interest rate of 0.015 per month. Use the payment function to compute the monthly payment. Position the cell pointer on cell D2. Type

PAYMENT

and press ⏎ to enter a cell label. Now position the cell pointer on cell E2. Type

@PMT(B2,.015,24)

and press ⏎ (Fig. 4.27). The value of the first argument, the amount of the loan, is found in cell B2. The other two arguments, interest rate and number of payments, are entered directly. The resulting monthly payment is displayed in cell E2.

Formulas involving functions are copied to other cells just like any formula. For example, follow the usual procedure to copy the formula in cell C11, @SUM(C6..C9), to cells D11 and E11. Position the cell pointer on cell C11. Press / C to choose the Copy menu option. Press ⏎ to accept the copy FROM range address C11..C11. Press →, . (period), and → to highlight the copy TO range address D11..E11. Press ⏎.

Position the cell pointer to cell D11 (Fig. 4.28) and study the copied formula. Notice that the range address for the @SUM function, D6..D9, has the same relative position to cell D11, since both C6 and C9 in the formula copied FROM are relative cell addresses.

Save the current worksheet as FINALBUD. A new example will be used in the following chapters.

```
D11: @SUM(D6..D9)                                                    READY
```

```
         A              B           C          D          E
1  BUDGET EXPENDITURE BY YEAR AND MONTH
2  ANNUAL INCOME      $30,000              PAYMENT      $1,498
3  ===========================================================
4  CATEGORY        PERCENTAGE    MONTHLY   QUARTERLY    ANNUAL
5  ===========================================================
6  HOUSING            30%         $750      $2,250      $9,000
7  FOOD               20%         $500      $1,500      $6,000
8  TRANSPORTATION     10%         $250        $750      $3,000
9  OTHER              40%       $1,000      $3,000     $12,000
10 ===========================================================
11 TOTAL                        $2,500      $7,500     $30,000
12
```

Figure 4.28 Copying formulas involving functions follows the same rules as copying any type of formulas. The formula in cell C11, @SUM(C6..C9), uses relative cell addresses. Thus when you copy it to D11 and E11, the cell addresses are adjusted to represent the same relative positions.

What Can Go Wrong?

1. You typed a function and pressed ⏎, and 1-2-3 beeped and put you in EDIT mode.

Cause: Something is wrong with the function: a misspelled name, an incorrect number of arguments, a blank space somewhere, or a missing parenthesis.

Solution: Use the EDIT mode keys to correct the function and press ⏎.

Summary

Function	Reference or keystrokes	Page
Absolute cell address	F4	93
Copy cell contents	/ C, range address FROM, ⏎, range address TO, ⏎	87
Functions, built-in	—	99
Functions, statistical	Fig. 4.26	100
Move cell contents	/ M, range address FROM, ⏎, range address TO, ⏎	95
Point, complete	⏎	81

102

Function	Reference or keystrokes	Page
Point, continue formula	Operator: + − * / ( )	85
Point, fix anchor cell	. (period)	82
Point, free anchor cell	[Esc]	82
Point, keys	⬅, ➡, ⬆, ⬇	81
Relative cell address	—	90

Self-Test

1. In pointing to a range address, the corner cell that remains fixed is called the _____ cell.

2. Press _____ to point to a cell 1 column to the right and press _____ to point to a cell 1 row up.

3. Press _____ to fix the anchor cell, and press _____ to free the anchor cell.

4. Many commands requiring a range address fix the location of the anchor cell at the position of the _____ when the command is activated.

5. When pointing to a cell address in a formula, press _____ to complete the formula and press _____ to continue the formula.

6. Suppose the contents of cell B2 are copied to cell C2. Indicate the new contents of cell C2 for each case given below:

   Contents of cell B2:   Contents of cell C2:

   a. "TOTALS   _____

   b. 13.45   _____

   c. +A1/12   _____

   d. +$A$1−3   _____

   e. +$A$2*A1   _____

7. If the copy FROM range is A1..E1 and the copy TO range is specified as B3, the implied copy TO range is _____.

8. In EDIT mode, press _____ to convert the cell address above the cursor to an absolute cell address.

9. The contents of cells A1, B1, and C1 are as follows: A1: +B1/2; B1: +A2*3; C1: "TITLE. If the contents of cell B1 are moved to C1, indicate the new contents of each of the cells.

   a. A1: _____

   b. B1: _____

   c. C1: _____

10. 1-2-3 functions begin with the _____ character.

11. The values contained in parentheses after the function name are called

   _____.

12. The contents of cells A1, B1, C1, and D1 contain the values 2, 4, 5, and 1, respectively. If the following functions are entered in cell A2, indicate the value displayed:

a. @SUM(B1..C1)   _____

b. @MAX(A1..D1)*2   _____

c. @MIN(A1..B1)/2   _____

Exercises

1. Print the worksheet you created by following the tutorial in this chapter (Fig. 4.28) and submit it to your instructor.

2. Retrieve the modified college budget worksheet that you created in Chapter 3. Erase part of the worksheet so that it looks like the one displayed below. Use POINT mode to define range and cell addresses.

```
COLLEGE BUDGET
ANNUAL EXPENDITURE     $9,600.00
=================================================================
CATEGORY                ANNUAL      SEMESTER      MONTH

TUITION                $4,800.00
HOUSING                $3,000.00
BOOKS                    $600.00
FRATERNITY               $300.00
CAR                      $300.00
OTHER
```

Use the shortcuts described in this chapter to create and modify this worksheet so it looks like the worksheet illustrated below. Enter cell formulas for SEMESTER and MONTH tuition. Enter a cell formula to compute the amount of money left over for OTHER expenses using the @SUM function. Complete the worksheet using the Copy command to duplicate cell information and using the Move command to rearrange the columns. Use the @SUM function to compute column totals. Print a copy of the completed worksheet.

```
COLLEGE BUDGET
ANNUAL EXPENDITURE     $9,600.00
=================================================================
CATEGORY                MONTH       SEMESTER      ANNUAL
=================================================================
TUITION                $400.00     $2,400.00    $4,800.00
HOUSING                $250.00     $1,500.00    $3,000.00
BOOKS                   $50.00       $300.00      $600.00
FRATERNITY              $25.00       $150.00      $300.00
CAR                     $25.00       $150.00      $300.00
OTHER                   $50.00       $300.00      $600.00
=================================================================
TOTALS                 $800.00     $4,800.00    $9,600.00
```

3. Retrieve the modified batting and slugging average worksheet that you created in Chapter 3. Erase part of the worksheet so that it looks like the one displayed below. Use POINT mode to define range and cell addresses.

```
BATTING AVERAGE COMPUTATION
=============================================================
RESULT                 FIRST HALF SECOND HALF        TOTAL
=============================================================
SINGLE                     8          4
DOUBLE                     2          2
TRIPLE                     2          0
HOME RUN                   1          1
OUT                       18         23
=============================================================
TOTAL AT BATS
=============================================================
BATTING AVERAGE
SLUGGING AVERAGE
```

Use the shortcuts described in this chapter to create and modify this worksheet so that it looks like the worksheet illustrated below. Use the @SUM function in all formulas computing totals. Enter a formula for TOTAL singles and copy it for each type of batting result. Enter a formula for TOTAL AT BATS, BATTING AVERAGE, SLUGGING AVERAGE, and OVER TEAM AVERAGE for the FIRST HALF. Copy these formulas all at once to the SECOND HALF and TOTAL columns. Format the cells in the new rows with the Fixed format with three decimal places.

```
BATTING AVERAGE COMPUTATION
=============================================================
RESULT                 FIRST HALF SECOND HALF        TOTAL
=============================================================
SINGLE                     8          4             12
DOUBLE                     2          2              4
TRIPLE                     2          0              2
HOME RUN                   1          1              2
OUT                       18         23             41
=============================================================
TOTAL AT BATS             31         30             61
=============================================================
BATTING AVERAGE        0.419      0.233          0.328
SLUGGING AVERAGE       0.710      0.400          0.557
OVER TEAM AVERAGE      0.119     -0.067          0.028

TEAM AVERAGE           0.300
```

5

Creating Worksheet Graphs

This chapter introduces the 1-2-3 features and commands that allow you to:

- create bar charts, line graphs, and pie charts based on worksheet data

- view these graphs on the screen

- add titles, axis labels, and legends to the graphs

- save a graph for printing

- learn additional graph features

Overview

At this point, you are familiar with the fundamentals necessary to create, modify, save, retrieve, and print an electronic spreadsheet efficiently. The remainder of the chapters are designed to introduce additional capabilities of 1-2-3. Generally, these are introduced at a fundamental level in the tutorial, and suggestions are made about related features that you might wish to investigate on your own. These additional investigations will build your confidence and allow you to learn features that are not covered in the tutorial.

The program name, 1-2-3, contains a double meaning. On one hand, the program is as easy to use as counting to 3. On the other hand, the program provides three major functions. Chapters 2, 3, and 4 provided a solid introduction to the first and most important function, the use of 1-2-3 as an **electronic spreadsheet**. This chapter introduces the second function, the use of 1-2-3 as a **graphing** program. Chapter 6 introduces the third function, the use of 1-2-3 as a **data management** program. Both graphing and data management require the creation of a worksheet before they are used. *Graphing requires a computer system with graphics capability and 1-2-3 configured to use this capability.* Ask for help if you're not sure your system has this capability.

The graphing tutorial in this chapter is based on the worksheet displayed in Fig. 5.1. This worksheet provides a quarterly projection of revenues and costs based on a sales forecast (row 3). Revenues (row 5) are computed by multiplying the sales forecast by the selling price ($5 per unit). The costs include a fixed component ($100 per quarter) and a variable component computed by multiplying the sales forecast by the variable cost ($3 per unit). The total costs (row 9) are computed by adding the fixed and variable components.

Begin the tutorial by creating this worksheet; refer to the fundamentals covered in Chapters 2–4. If you have difficulty, use the steps outlined below. Use POINT mode whenever possible. Keystrokes required to select appropriate menu options are listed in parentheses.

1. Enter labels in the following cells:

A1: QUARTERLY REVENUE/COST PROJECTION:

A3: SALES (units)

A5: REVENUES ($5/unit)

A10: [W24]   READY

	A	B	C	D	E
1	QUARTERLY REVENUE/COST PROJECTION:				
2		QTR 1	QTR 2	QTR 3	QTR 4
3	SALES (units)	100	200	150	80
4					
5	REVENUES ($5/unit)	$500	$1,000	$750	$400
6					
7	FIXED COSTS ($100/qtr)	$100	$100	$100	$100
8	VARIABLE COSTS ($3/unit)	$300	$600	$450	$240
9	TOTAL COSTS	$400	$700	$550	$340
10					

Figure 5.1 Create this worksheet for the graphing tutorial.

Creating Worksheet Graphs
Overview

107

A7: FIXED COSTS ($100/qtr)

A8: VARIABLE COSTS ($3/unit)

A9: TOTAL COSTS

B2: QTR 1

C2: QTR 2

D2: QTR 3

E2: QTR 4

2. Enter numbers in the following cells:

B3: 100

C3: 200

D3: 150

E3: 80

B7: 100

3. Enter formulas in the following cells:

B5: 5*B3

B8: 3*B3

B9: +B7+B8

4. Copy the contents of cells B5..B9 to cells C5..E9 (/ C)

5. Set the global column width to 12 (/ W G C)

6. Set the column width of A to 24 (/ W C S)

7. Set the format of B5..E9 to Currency with 0 decimal places (/ R F)

8. Align the labels in B2..E2 with the right edge of the cell (/ R L R)

9. Save the worksheet, using the file name GRAPHEX (/ F S)

Types of Graphs

A **graph** is a way of visually representing some numeric information. For example, row 5 of the tutorial worksheet contains revenue values for each quarter of the upcoming year. These may be pictured as a **line graph**, a **bar graph**, or a **pie chart** (Fig. 5.2).

The line graph and the bar graph are graphs in which the horizontal axis (X-axis) contains a label to indicate the quarter represented and the vertical axis (Y-axis) contains a point or bar proportional to the numeric value represented. The pie chart provides a label (similar to the X-axis label) and a slice

a) Line graph

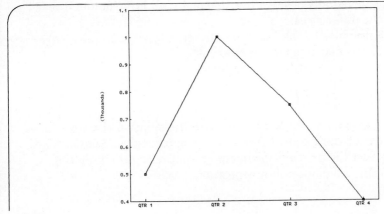

b) Pie chart

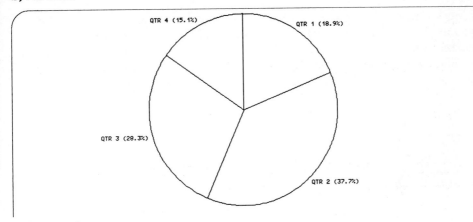

c) Bar graph

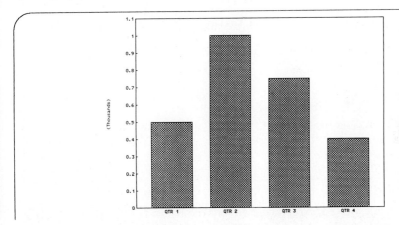

Figure 5.2 Three types of graphs are used to represent quarterly revenues.

of pie proportional to the numeric value in each quarter. All of these graphs allow the viewer to visually observe the quarters with large or small revenues and the size of the differences.

Though 1-2-3 provides the ability to create other types of graphs, only these three types are discussed in the tutorial.

Creating Graphs

Creating graphs with 1-2-3 begins with the creation of a worksheet containing the data to be graphed. You did this in a previous section. The next step is to select the primary menu option containing the graphing functions. With the cell pointer in any position, press

/ G
└─ Graph

Line 2 of the control panel lists the available graphing menu options, and if you are using Release 2.2, the worksheet is replaced with a table listing the current graph settings (Fig. 5.3). This menu will be called the **Graph menu**.

The Graph menu is a "sticky" menu. When you select an option from this menu, you'll return to the menu rather than to READY mode as you did with

```
A10: [W24]                                                           MENU
Type  X  A  B  C  D  E  F  Reset  View  Save  Options  Name  Group  Quit
Line  Bar  XY  Stack-Bar  Pie
┌──────────────────────── Graph Settings ─────────────────────────┐
│  Type: Line              Titles: First                          │
│                                  Second                         │
│  X:                              X axis                         │
│  A:                              Y axis                         │
│  B:                                                             │
│  C:                                        Y scale:    X scale: │
│  D:                              Scaling   Automatic   Automatic│
│  E:                              Lower                          │
│  F:                              Upper                          │
│                                  Format    (G)        (G)       │
│  Grid: None      Color: No       Indicator Yes        Yes       │
│                                                                 │
│     Legend:          Format:  Data labels:        Skip: 1       │
│  A                   Both                                       │
│  B                   Both                                       │
│  C                   Both                                       │
│  D                   Both                                       │
│  E                   Both                                       │
│  F                   Both                                       │
└─────────────────────────────────────────────────────────────────┘
```

Figure 5.3 Line 2 lists the graphing menu options available in 1-2-3, and the table displays the current graph settings. Select Quit to return to READY mode.

Menu Choice	Provides Options for
Type	specifying the type of graph to draw
X	specifying the labels or values for the X-axis
A–F	specifying one to six sets of values to be represented on the Y-axis
Reset	clearing previously specified graph settings
View	viewing the currently specified graph
Save	saving the currently specified graph for later printing
Options	enhancing the appearance of a graph
Name	naming and saving multiple graph specifications as a part of the worksheet
Group	specifying the X values and all sets of data values (A–F) at once
Quit	returning to READY mode

Figure 5.4 The Graph option in 1-2-3 provides options for creating graphs based on numeric data in the worksheet.

previous menus. The only way to leave the Graph menu and return to READY mode is to select the menu option Quit.

Press ⊡ to highlight each of the menu options and read the descriptions on line 3. Compare these with the descriptions in Fig. 5.4 to get an idea of what graphing functions are available. In the tutorial you'll use Type, X, A, B, View, Save and Options from this menu. Leave the Graph menu displayed as you continue the tutorial.

Keystroke Summary: Access the Graph menu

Press: / G
          └── Graph

Select: *one or more Graph menu options*

Press: Q
          └── Quit

Defining Values to Graph

The first step in creating a graph is to define a range address that contains a set of numeric values to be represented on the graph. The first value in the range is graphed in the first graph position, the second value in the second position, and so on. Up to six sets of values (named A, B, C, D, E, F) may be represented on a single line graph or bar graph (this is illustrated later). The pie chart may represent only one set of values.

To define data set A to be the quarterly revenue values, press

A
└── A (Set A)

You are prompted to define the range address containing the numeric values to be graphed:

    Enter first data range: A10

Use POINT mode to define the range address containing the quarterly revenues; highlight cell B5 using the cursor keys, press . (period) to fix the anchor cell, and highlight the range address B5..E5 (Fig. 5.5). Press ⏎.

The graph settings table indicates that data set A is contained in range address B5..E5 of the worksheet. This includes the four numeric values 500, 1000, 750, and 400. These are used to position points on a line graph, to determine the height of bars on a bar graph, and to determine the angle width on a pie chart.

Keystroke Summary: Define values to graph

From the Graph menu (/ G):

Press: A or B or C or D or E or F
          └──┴──┴──┴──┴──┴── Six data sets

Type or
  point: *range address*

Press: ⏎

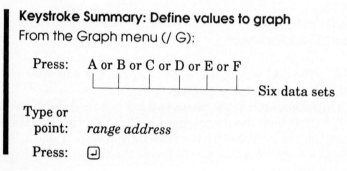

```
E5: (C0) 5*E3                                                    POINT
Enter first data range: B5..E5
```

	A	B	C	D	E
1	QUARTERLY REVENUE/COST PROJECTION:				
2		QTR 1	QTR 2	QTR 3	QTR 4
3	SALES (units)	100	200	150	80
4					
5	REVENUES ($5/unit)	$500	$1,000	$750	$400
6					
7	FIXED COSTS ($100/qtr)	$100	$100	$100	$100
8	VARIABLE COSTS ($3/unit)	$300	$600	$450	$240
9	TOTAL COSTS	$400	$700	$550	$340
10					

Figure 5.5 The quarterly revenue values in range address B5..E5 are the first set of values (set A) on the graph.

Defining Value Identifiers

The second step is to define a range address that contains a set of labels or numeric values that are used to identify the values on the graph. The first identifier is associated with the first value graphed, the second identifier with the second value, and so on. These identifiers appear on the X-axis of a line graph or bar graph and outside the wedges on a pie chart.

The column labels on the tutorial worksheet, QTR 1, QTR 2, QTR 3, and QTR 4, provide a convenient set of identifiers for the values to be graphed. To select these, press

X
└── X (X-axis)

You are prompted as follows:

```
Enter x-axis range: A10
```

Use POINT mode to enter the range address B2..E2 (Fig. 5.6) and press ↵.

You have now defined QTR 1 as the identifier for 500, QTR 2 as the identifier for 1000, and so on. The graph settings table indicates that the X labels are in range address B2..E2.

> **Keystroke Summary: Define value identifiers**
>
> From the Graph menu (/ G):
>
> Press: X
>   └──── X-axis or pie chart labels
>
> Type or
> point: *range address*
>
> Press: ↵

```
E2: "QTR 4                                                        POINT
Enter x-axis range: B2..E2
```

	A	B	C	D	E
1	QUARTERLY REVENUE/COST PROJECTION:				
2		QTR 1	QTR 2	QTR 3	QTR 4
3	SALES (units)	100	200	150	80
4					
5	REVENUES ($5/unit)	$500	$1,000	$750	$400
6					
7	FIXED COSTS ($100/qtr)	$100	$100	$100	$100
8	VARIABLE COSTS ($3/unit)	$300	$600	$450	$240
9	TOTAL COSTS	$400	$700	$550	$340
10					

Figure 5.6 The column labels in range address B2..E2 are identifiers for the data values on the graph.

Viewing the Graph

Once you have defined the values to graph and a set of identifiers, press

to display the graph on the screen. The graph settings table disappears, and a line graph (Fig. 5.2a) fills the entire screen. 1-2-3 automatically defines a scale for the Y-axis and represents the revenues and associated identifiers on the graph.

When you have finished inspecting the graph, press any key and you're back to the Graph menu.

Your computer system must have graphics capability to display graphs on the screen. You may create and print graphs without this capability, but you will not be able to use the View feature.

> **Keystroke Summary: View a graph**
> From the Graph menu (/G):
>
> Press: V
>   └── View
>
> Press: *Any key*

Selecting the Graph Type

The numeric values in the data set may be represented by using several different types of graphs. The line graph obtained in the last section is the default. Press

T
└── Type

to select another type of graph. Line 2 of the control panel provides the following choices:

```
Line  Bar  XY  Stack-Bar  Pie
```

Press P to select a pie chart.

To see the new graph, press V. The quarterly revenues are now displayed as a pie chart (Fig. 5.2b). Press any key to return to the Graph menu.

Continue the tutorial by changing to a bar graph; press T B. Press V to view the bar graph on the screen (Fig. 5.2c). This is probably the most visually informative graph for this data set. Press a key to return to the Graph menu. The View feature allows you to look at several types of graphs and select the most informative.

You will be given the opportunity to explore the other graph types later in this chapter.

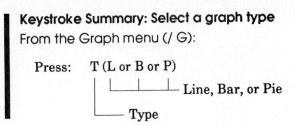

Defining Multiple Sets of Values to Graph

It was pointed out earlier that up to six sets of values may be represented on a single line graph or bar graph. This is illustrated below by graphing the quarterly total costs along with the quarterly revenues.

Data set A is defined as the quarterly revenues. Press

B
└── B (Set B)

to define a set of numeric values for data set B. In response to the prompt

    Enter second data range: A10

use POINT mode to select range address B9..E9 (Fig. 5.7). Press ↵. Data set B now contains the four total cost values 400, 700, 550, and 340, corresponding to the X identifiers QTR 1, QTR 2, QTR 3, and QTR 4, respectively.

Press V to view the bar graph with two sets of data values (Fig. 5.8). The single bar in Fig. 5.2c is replaced with a pair of bars, one for each data set defined. Data set A (revenues) is the left bar and data set B (total costs) is the right bar. This type of graph is useful to compare sets of numeric values. Press any key to return to the Graph menu.

```
E9: (C0) +E7+E8                                              POINT
Enter second data range: B9..E9
```

	A	B	C	D	E
1	QUARTERLY REVENUE/COST PROJECTION:				
2		QTR 1	QTR 2	QTR 3	QTR 4
3	SALES (units)	100	200	150	80
4					
5	REVENUES ($5/unit)	$500	$1,000	$750	$400
6					
7	FIXED COSTS ($100/qtr)	$100	$100	$100	$100
8	VARIABLE COSTS ($3/unit)	$300	$600	$450	$240
9	TOTAL COSTS	$400	$700	$550	$340
10					

Figure 5.7 The quarterly total costs in range address B9..E9 are the second set of values (set B) on the graph.

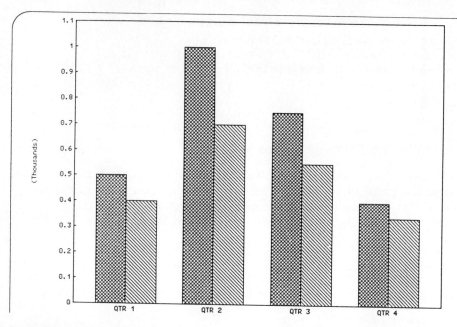

Figure 5.8 Quarterly revenues (left bar) and quarterly total costs (right bar) are displayed side by side on the same bar graph.

Four additional data sets may be defined by selecting menu options C, D, E, and F. See the Keystroke Summary in the section on Defining Data Values to Graph.

What Can Go Wrong?

1. You pressed V to view a graph, and the computer beeped and the screen went blank.

Cause: You have not defined a set of data values to graph.

Solution: Press any key to return to the Graph menu. Press A to define a set of data values to graph.

2. Your graph appears to have the wrong data values when compared to the illustrations.

Cause: You pointed to the wrong range address when defining the A or B data set. If the range address includes any labels, these are graphed as a numeric value of 0.

Solution: Press any key to return to the graphing menu options. Select menu option A or B as appropriate, and correct the range address. If the anchor cell is wrong, press ⌷Esc⌷ and define the complete range address. If the anchor cell is correct, use the cursor keys to highlight the appropriate range. Press ⏎ and view the graph again.

3. You selected the XY graph type, and when you viewed the graph, all of the points are on the Y-axis.

Cause: The XY graph is similar to the line graph except that the values in the X range must be numeric and are positioned on the X-axis according to their numeric value. In the tutorial the X range contains labels. These labels are assigned the value 0, and thus all points on the graph are on the Y-axis.

Solution: Press any key to return to the graphing menu options. Select menu option T to change the Type. The XY graph is not appropriate for the X range specified.

Labeling Graphs

The graphs created in the previous section are useful for seeing relationships between numeric values, but they are not ready to show to anyone else. They need to be labeled so that the viewer will know what is represented. 1-2-3 provides a number of menu options for labeling and improving the appearance of graphs.

These menu options are accessed through the graphing menu choice called Options. Press

O
└── Options

Line 2 of the control panel (Fig. 5.9) displays a list of these options. This is also a "sticky" menu and will be called the **Graph Options menu**. Press ⊟ to highlight each menu option and read the description on line 3 to familiarize yourself with some of the choices available. To return to the Graph menu, select the option Quit.

```
A10: [W24]                                                        MENU
Legend  Format  Titles  Grid  Scale  Color  B&W  Data-Labels  Quit
Create legends for data ranges
```

Figure 5.9 Line 2 of the control panel lists the menu choices in the Graph Options menu. These options are used to label and enhance the appearance of a graph.

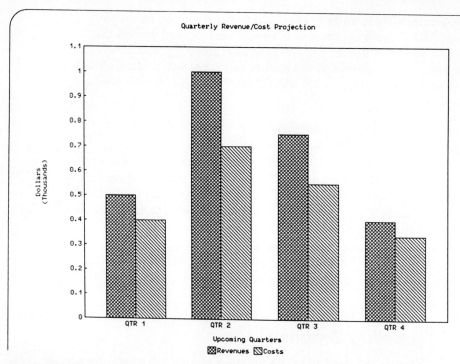

Figure 5.10 The bar chart in Fig. 5.8 is finished by including a title, axis labels, and a legend.

In this section of the tutorial you will label the previously created graph so that it appears as in Fig. 5.10. The option called Titles is used to place the title at the top of the graph and to label each axis. The option called Legend is used to create the key at the bottom of the graph indicating what each bar represents.

Keystroke Summary: Access the Graph Options menu
From the Graph menu (/ G):

Press: O
       └── Options

Select: *one or more Graph Options choices*

Press: Q
       └── Quit

Titles and Axis Labels

Begin by placing a title at the top of the graph. From the Graph Options menu, press

to define the first (of possibly two) line of the title. In response to the prompt

        Enter first line of graph title:

type

        Quarterly Revenue/Cost Projection

Press ⏎ to return to the Graph Options menu.
    Next, specify a label for the Y-axis. Press

Answer the prompt

        Enter y-axis title:

by typing

        Dollars

Press ⏎ to complete this process.
    Similarly, define the X-axis label by pressing

and typing

        Upcoming Quarters

in response to the prompt. Press ⏎. Note that all of the titles and labels specified are listed in the graph settings table.
    View the graph to confirm that the changes have taken place. Press Q (for Quit) to return to the Graph menu. Press V to view the graph. The graph now includes a one-line title, a Y-axis label, and an X-axis label as in Fig. 5.10 (the legend at the bottom has not been specified yet). Press any key to return to the Graph menu.

Legends

Continue the tutorial by defining a **legend** to indicate the meaning of each type of bar on the graph. Press O to return to the Graph Options menu. Press

L

└── Legend

to specify a graph legend. Line 2 of the control panel displays

```
A B C D E F Range
```

so that you may choose a legend for one of the data sets. Press A to specify a legend for the quarterly revenue data. In response to the prompt

```
Enter legend for first data range:
```

type

```
Revenues
```

Press ⏎, and the legend for data set A is defined.

Follow a similar procedure to create a legend for data set B. Press L B and type

```
Costs
```

in response to the prompt. Press ⏎.

Now view the graph again. Press Q to return to the Graph menu followed by V to view the currently defined graph. The graph now includes the legend as in Fig. 5.10.

120

What Can Go Wrong?

1. You're looking for the View option to display your graph but can't seem to find it.

Cause: Remember that the Graph menu and Graph Options menu are "sticky" menus. When an option is selected from these menus, you're returned to the same menu. You are probably in the Graph Options menu.

Solution: Press Q (for Quit) to leave this "sticky" menu and return to the Graph menu, which contains View.

2. You have made some major mistakes in creating your graph and would like to cancel all settings and start over.

Cause: You made some incorrect menu selections.

Solution: Return to the main Graph menu. You may already be there, or you may need to press Q to leave the Graph Options menu.

Press: R G Q

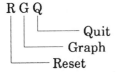

Quit
Graph
Reset

to cancel all the graph settings.

Saving Graphs

Once you have created and labeled a graph, you'll want to save it on a disk. Separate procedures are required to save a graph for screen viewing and for printing.

Saving a Graph for Screen Viewing

Saving a graph for screen viewing is simple. Whenever a worksheet is saved, all the settings for the current graph are automatically saved as part of the worksheet. Simply save the worksheet, using the procedures you learned in Chapter 2.

Press Q to exit the Graph menu and return to READY mode. Press / F S to resave the worksheet. On a hard disk system, Line 2 will display the prompt

```
Enter save file name: C:\123DATA\GRAPHEX.WK1
```

indicating that you previously saved the worksheet on the hard drive (C), in directory 123DATA, using the file name GRAPHEX. (A similar prompt will appear on a floppy disk system.) Press ⏎ to accept the file name, and press R to replace the previous version of GRAPHEX.

The settings for the graph in Fig. 5.10 are saved with the worksheet. You may later retrieve this worksheet and press / G V to view the graph.

Saving a Graph for Printing

Obtaining a printed copy of a graph is a two step process. First, the graph must be saved in a special disk file for printing. Then you must exit 1-2-3 and load another program, PrintGraph, to print the graph. PrintGraph reads the special disk file and prints the graph. The tutorial illustrates the procedure for saving a graph for printing, and Appendix D describes how to load and run PrintGraph.

Press / G to return to the Graph menu. Press

to select the menu option to save a graph for later printing. Respond to the prompt

```
Enter graph file name: C:\123DATA\*.pic
```

by typing

BARCHART

Press ↵. The disk file BARCHART can now be accessed by the PrintGraph program to obtain a printed copy of the graph.

Note that the file BARCHART contains only information for printing the graph. BARCHART may not be retrieved or used by 1-2-3.

> **Keystroke Summary: Save a graph for printing**
> From the Graph menu (/ G):
>
> Press: S
>   └── Save
>
> Type: *file name*
>
> Press: ↵

Other Graphing Features

There is not enough space to cover all of the graphing functions in detail in this tutorial. However, you are encouraged to explore some of the other graphing features on your own. You know how to use the menu system. Try some options that were not covered in the tutorial. Watch the control panel for information and prompts. If you have difficulty, press [Esc] to back out of a menu choice and start over. Also, use the 1-2-3 reference manual; consult the chapter that describes graph commands.

Some 1-2-3 graphing capabilities that you might wish to explore are listed below. Some of these are accessed from the Graph menu and others from the Graph Options menu. Try each one and view the graph to see what happens. The menu option name is included in parentheses.

From the Graph menu (/ G):

1. *Other graph types:* In addition to the graph types discussed in the tutorial, data may be represented by using a stacked bar graph and an XY plot. If you try an XY plot, change the X range to a set of numeric values. (Type)

2. *Specify shading on a pie chart:* Use data set B to specify the shading to be used in a pie chart. (B)

3. *Save multiple graphs with the worksheet:* To save more than one graph with the worksheet, the graphs must be assigned names. Named graphs may be declared current and deleted. (Name)

4. *Specify multiple data ranges at once:* If the X and A–F data ranges are in consecutive columns or rows, they may be specified together by using this feature. (Group, Release 2.2 only)

From the Graph Options menu (/ G O):

1. *Specify the format of Line and XY graphs:* Line and XY graphs may include lines only, points only, or lines and points. (Format)

2. *Include a grid on the graph:* All graph types except the pie chart may contain horizontal, vertical, or both types of grid lines. (Grid)

3. *Specify axis scaling:* The Y-axis and the X-axis (on an XY graph) are normally scaled automatically, but you can control the scaling manually if you wish. (Scale)

4. *Color or black and white:* If you have a color monitor, you may specify color for your graph. Otherwise, choose black and white. (Color and B&W)

5. *Label data points on the graph:* All graph types except the pie chart may include labels for individual points or bars on the graph. (Label)

Summary

Function	Reference or Keystrokes	Page
Graph, access menu	/ G	110
Graph, define axis labels	(/ G O) T, X or Y, label, ⏎	119
Graph, define legend	(/ G O) L, A or B or C or D or E or F, legend, ⏎	120
Graph, define title	(/ G O) T, F or S, title, ⏎	119

Function	Reference or Keystrokes	Page
Graph, define values	(/ G) A or B or C or D or E or F, range address, ↵	111
Graph, define X values	(/ G) X, range address, ↵	113
Graph, options menu	(/ G) O	117
Graph, select type	(/ G) T, L or B or P	114
Graph, view	(/ G) V	114
Print a graph	Appendix D	179
Save a graph to print	(/ G) S, file name, ↵	122
Save a graph to view	/ F S, file name, ↵	121
Sticky menu	—	110
Sticky menu exit	Q	111

Self-Test

1. 1-2-3 provides three major functions: _____, _____, and _____.

2. Press _____ to select the Graph menu, and press _____ to select the Graph Options menu.

3. The Graph menu and the Graph Options menu are called _____ menus because when a menu action is complete, you return to the menu rather than to READY mode.

4. A line graph and a bar graph may display up to _____ data sets, but a pie chart may display only _____ data set.

5. Press _____ from the Graph menu to define the numeric values in range address B1..E1 as the values for data set A.

6. Press _____ from the Graph menu to define the contents of cells in range address B2..E2 as identifiers for the X axis of a line graph.

7. Press _____ from the Graph menu to view the currently defined graph.

8. Press _____ from the Graph menu to change the graph type to a pie chart.

9. Press _____ from the Graph Options menu to enter the title PLOT OF QUARTERLY SALES at the top of the graph.

10. Press _____ from the Graph Options menu to create the label QUARTER for the X-axis of a bar graph.

11. Press _____ from the Graph Options menu to define the legend SALES for data set B.

12. Press _____ from the Graph menu to save a graph in the file name PLOT for later printing.

Exercises

1. Save a copy of the line graph, the bar graph, and the pie chart in Fig. 5.2 for printing. Print a copy of these graphs and submit them to your instructor. Also save, print, and submit a copy of the graph in Fig. 5.10.

2. Use the graphing tutorial worksheet to create the following graph.

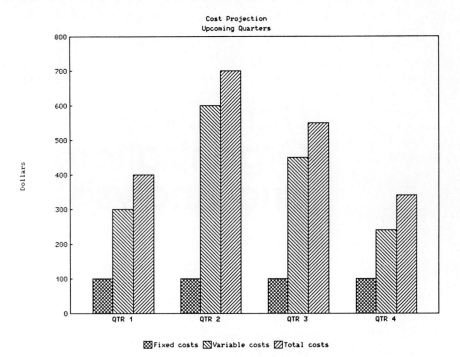

3. Use the MODBUDGT worksheet from the tutorial in Chapter 3 to create the following graph. The shading is optional. (To obtain shading, enter the values 1, 2, 3, and 4 in adjacent cells and define this range as data set B.)

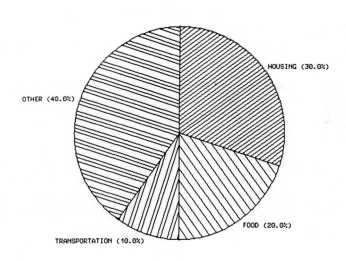

6

Data Entry, Organization, and Analysis

This chapter introduces the 1-2-3 features and commands that allow you to:

- organize portions of a worksheet as a database
- enter a sequence of numbers in a worksheet
- reorder records in a worksheet
- search a worksheet database for particular records
- learn additional data analysis features

Creating a Worksheet Database

You have learned to use 1-2-3 to create worksheets and to create graphs of selected values from the worksheet. In this chapter you'll learn to enter, organize, and analyze data in a worksheet. Data management is 1-2-3's third major capability.

Some of the capabilities discussed in this chapter require that portions of the worksheet be organized as a "database." Fig. 6.1 illustrates a **worksheet database**. This database contains information about a group of university faculty members for the past year. The data include the name of

	A	B	C	D	E	F
1	NAME	DEPARTMENT	CREDIT HRS	GRANT DOLRS		
2	Baker	Business	24	$0		
3	Troy	Math	23	$0		
4	Smith	Math	17	$30,000		
5	Waller	Physics	16	$15,000		
6	Miller	Business	19	$8,000		
7	Scott	Business	25	$0		
8	Hall	History	22	$0		
9	Edwards	Physics	16	$12,000		
10	Taylor	Business	21	$5,000		
11	Davis	Math	23	$0		
12	Hooper	Chemistry	20	$10,000		
13						

Figure 6.1 Create the worksheet above. It is organized as a 1-2-3 database.

the faculty member, the university department, the number of credit hours taught, and the number of grant dollars obtained. In the language of data management, each data element (name, department, and so on) is called a **field**. All the fields for a particular faculty member (for example, row 2, which contains all the fields for Baker) is called a **record**, and all the records in this group constitute a **file**. Commands are available in 1-2-3 to sort the records in a database and to search the database for certain records.

A portion of a worksheet is organized as a database by using the following conventions.

1. Use a worksheet column for each field.

2. Use a worksheet row for each record.

3. Use the first row of the database range to establish a name for each field. (In Fig. 6.1, the field name for column A is NAME, the field name for column B is DEPARTMENT, and so on.)

4. Do not leave any blank records or dividers in the database range.

Begin the tutorial by creating the database worksheet in Fig. 6.1. Follow the steps listed below.

1. Enter field names as labels in row 1. Capitalize these field names to distinguish them from field data.

2. Enter data for each record in rows 2–12. Columns A and B are labels, and columns C and D are numbers.

3. Set the global column width to 12. (/ W G C)

4. Set the format of D2..D12 to Currency with 0 decimal places. (/ R F)

5. Save the worksheet using the file name DATAEX. (/ F S)

```
A13:
Fill  Table  Sort  Query  Distribution  Matrix  Regression  Parse
Fill a range with a sequence of values
```

Figure 6.2 Line 2 lists the menu options available in the Data group.

Menu options to enter, organize, and analyze worksheet data are accessed from the primary menu option Data. Press

/ D
└─ Data

The data management menu options are listed on line 2 of the control panel (Fig. 6.2). Familiarize yourself with the listed options by pressing ⊡ to highlight each option so that you can read the descriptions on line 3. Compare these descriptions with those provided in Fig. 6.3.

Some of these commands are used to enter worksheet data (Fill, Parse), some are used to analyze data (Table, Distribution, Matrix, and Regression),

Menu Choice	Provides Options for
Fill	entering a sequence of numbers in a worksheet
Table	producing a table of numeric results obtained by varying one or two values in a worksheet formula
Sort	rearranging the rows of a worksheet or the records of a worksheet database
Query	selecting records from a database with certain characteristics
Distribution	creating a frequency distribution from a range of numbers
Matrix	multiplying and inverting matrices
Regression	computing linear regression coefficients based on worksheet data
Parse	dividing a column of long labels into several columns

Figure 6.3 The Data option in 1-2-3 provides options for data entry, data organization, and analysis. The Query option requires the worksheet data to be organized as a database.

and some are used to organize and search a worksheet database (Sort and Query). You'll use the Fill, Sort, and Query options in the tutorial and be given the opportunity to explore some of the others on your own. Press ⎋Esc to return to READY mode.

Entering Number Sequences

1-2-3 provides a handy feature for entering a **sequence** of numbers in a worksheet range. A sequence begins with a Start number, is incremented by a Step size, and ends with a Stop number. The number sequence (2,5,8,11,14,17) *starts* with 2, *steps* by 3, and *stops* at 17.

To illustrate, add a field to the database worksheet that contains the sequence number of the records as illustrated in Fig. 6.4. Position the cell pointer on cell E1 and type

SEQUENCE NO

to create a new field name.

Rather than type in the sequence numbers one at a time, press

to choose the Data option to Fill in a sequence of numbers. In response to the prompt

```
Enter fill range: E1
```

E1: 'SEQUENCE NO   `READY`

	A	B	C	D	E	F
1	NAME	DEPARTMENT	CREDIT HRS	GRANT DOLRS	SEQUENCE NO	
2	Baker	Business	24	$0	1	
3	Troy	Math	23	$0	2	
4	Smith	Math	17	$30,000	3	
5	Waller	Physics	16	$15,000	4	
6	Miller	Business	19	$8,000	5	
7	Scott	Business	25	$0	6	
8	Hall	History	22	$0	7	
9	Edwards	Physics	16	$12,000	8	
10	Taylor	Business	21	$5,000	9	
11	Davis	Math	23	$0	10	
12	Hooper	Chemistry	20	$10,000	11	

Figure 6.4 The new field, SEQUENCE NO, contains the position number of each record in the worksheet database. These data values will be entered by using the Data Fill menu option.

POINT to the range address E2..E12. The anchor cell is free, so position the cell pointer at E2, press . (period), and highlight the desired range. Press ⏎.

You'll be prompted on line 3 to enter the beginning sequence number:

> Start: 0

A default value of 0 is assumed. Type

> 1

and press ⏎ to select a starting sequence number of 1.

Another prompt will appear in the middle of line 3:

> Step: 1

Press ⏎ to accept the default step size of 1.

Finally, a third prompt will appear on the right of line 3:

> Stop: 8191

Fig. 6.5 displays the current screen. The default value, 8191, indicates that a sequence of numbers will be generated up to 8191 or until the range address is filled. In your case, the range address will be filled at 11. So press ⏎ to accept the default value, and the sequence numbers will be filled in as desired (Fig. 6.4).

Keystroke Summary: Enter a number sequence

Press: / D F
                    └── Fill
                └── Data

Type or
point: *range address*

Press: ⏎

Type: *starting number*

Press: ⏎

Type: *step size*

Press: ⏎

Type: *stopping number*

Press: ⏎

```
E1: 'SEQUENCE NO                                                    EDIT
Enter fill range: E2..E12
Start: 1                    Step: 1              Stop: 8191
```

Figure 6.5 You must specify the range address, the starting value, the step size, and the stopping value to Fill a sequence of numbers in the worksheet.

Sorting Data

Sorting is the process of placing data or database records in a fixed order. For example, the records in the tutorial database may be alphabetized by name, alphabetized by department, or placed in descending order by credit hours taught. Sorting is an important data management function because fixing the order makes information easier to find.

Position the cell pointer at cell A2 and press

```
/ D S
    └── Sort
  └── Data
```

to access the 1-2-3 **Data Sort menu** (Fig. 6.6). This is another "sticky" menu. To return to READY mode, press G (for Go) to go ahead and sort the data, or press Q (for Quit) to leave this menu without sorting.

In the tutorial, you will organize the database records so that the departments appear in alphabetical order and the faculty members in each department are ordered by credit hours taught, from highest to lowest (Fig. 6.7).

Sorting is a three-step process. First, the data or database records to be sorted must be defined by using the Data-Range menu option. Second, a sorting key must be established. A **key** is the data value (or field) that is used to order the data. 1-2-3 allows one or two keys by selecting menu option Primary-Key and Secondary-Key. The third step is to proceed with the sort by selecting menu option Go.

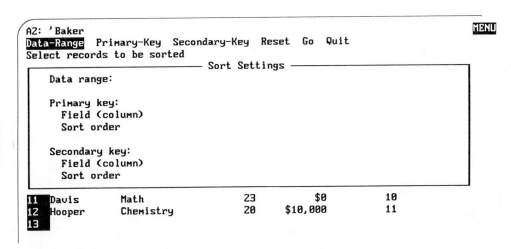

Figure 6.6 Line 2 lists the menu choices on the Data Sort menu. With Release 2.2 the current sort settings are displayed in a table overlaying the worksheet.

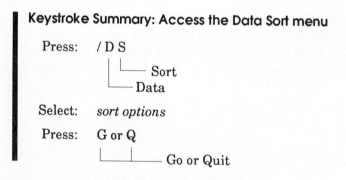

	A	B	C	D	E	F
1	NAME	DEPARTMENT	CREDIT HRS	GRANT DOLRS	SEQUENCE NO	
2	Scott	Business	25	$0	6	
3	Baker	Business	24	$0	1	
4	Taylor	Business	21	$5,000	9	
5	Miller	Business	19	$8,000	5	
6	Hooper	Chemistry	20	$10,000	11	
7	Hall	History	22	$0	7	
8	Davis	Math	23	$0	10	
9	Troy	Math	23	$0	2	
10	Smith	Math	17	$30,000	3	
11	Waller	Physics	16	$15,000	4	
12	Edwards	Physics	16	$12,000	8	

Figure 6.7 The records in the worksheet database are placed in alphabetical order by DEPARTMENT (Primary-Key). Within each department, the records are ordered by CREDIT HRS (Secondary-Key) from highest to lowest.

Keystroke Summary: Access the Data Sort menu

Press: / D S

         └──── Sort
         └── Data

Select: *sort options*

Press: G or Q

         └──┴── Go or Quit

Defining Data to be Sorted

From the Data Sort menu, press

D
 └── Data-Range

to specify the database records to be sorted. You'll be prompted as follows:

    Enter data range: A2

Specify a range address that includes all of the records to be sorted and all of the fields associated with each record. Do not include the row of field names in the range of data to be sorted. POINT to range address A2..E12 (Fig. 6.8) and press ⏎. With Release 2.2 the specified data range will be displayed in the sort settings table.

	A	B	C	D	E	F
1	NAME	DEPARTMENT	CREDIT HRS	GRANT DOLRS	SEQUENCE NO	
2	Baker	Business	24	$0	1	
3	Troy	Math	23	$0	2	
4	Smith	Math	17	$30,000	3	
5	Waller	Physics	16	$15,000	4	
6	Miller	Business	19	$8,000	5	
7	Scott	Business	25	$0	6	
8	Hall	History	22	$0	7	
9	Edwards	Physics	16	$12,000	8	
10	Taylor	Business	21	$5,000	9	
11	Davis	Math	23	$0	10	
12	Hooper	Chemistry	20	$10,000	11	

Figure 6.8 The Data-Range address includes all records to be sorted and all fields associated with these records.

> **Keystroke Summary: Define sort data**
>
> From the Data Sort menu (/ D S):
>
> Press: D
>   └── Data-Range
>
> Type or
> point: *range address*
>
> Press: ↵

Selecting Sorting Keys

Next, specify the DEPARTMENT as the primary sorting key. From the Data Sort menu, press

P
└── Primary-Key

You'll be prompted as follows:

    Primary sort key: A2

Enter any cell address in the field (or column) that contains the values to be used in ordering the records. For example, point to cell B2 to specify the DEPARTMENT as the key. Press ↵.

In response to the prompt on the right side of line 2 (Fig. 6.9):

    Sort order (A or D): D

type A and press ↵ to sort in ascending (alphabetical) order.

> **Data Entry, Organization, and Analysis**   **133**
> **Sorting Data**

```
A2: 'Baker                                                          EDIT
Primary sort key: B2              Sort order (A or D): A
```

Figure 6.9 The Primary-Key contains a cell address in the field (or column) to be used in ordering the records. Specify A for ascending order or D for descending order. Similarly, a Secondary-Key may be specified.

To order the faculty members within each department by credit hours taught, specify CREDIT HRS as the secondary sort key. Press

S
└── Secondary-Key

POINT to cell address C2 in response to the prompt

    Secondary sort key: A2

Press ⏎.

Answer the prompt

    Sort order (A or D): A

by typing D for descending order, and press ⏎. You have specified that the faculty records within each department will be ordered from highest to lowest according to the number of credit hours taught. With Release 2.2 the primary and secondary key information is displayed in the sort settings table.

> **Keystroke Summary: Define sort keys**
> From the Data Sort menu (/ D S):
>
> Press: P or S
>   └──┴── Primary-Key or Secondary-Key
>
> Type or
>   point: *range address*
>
> Press: ⏎
>
> Type: A or D (ascending or descending order)
>
> Press: ⏎

Sorting Records

Now that you have defined the records to be sorted and the sorting keys to be used, press

G
└── Go

134

to perform the sorting operation. You'll be returned to READY mode with the records in the database rearranged as in Fig. 6.7.

Notice that the sequence numbers show the original position of each record. For additional practice, use these to return the records to their original order. Press / D S to return to the Sort menu. Press P and select E2, representing the SEQUENCE NO field, as the Primary-Key. Type A to choose ascending order, and Press ⏎. Press G to sort the records back to their original order (Fig. 6.4). Note that it is not necessary to define the data to be sorted in this case, since you defined them previously.

> **Keystroke Summary: Sort records**
> From the Data Sort menu (/ D S):
>
> Press: G
>   └── Go

What Can Go Wrong?

1. You pressed G (for Go) to sort the database records, the computer beeped, and nothing happened.

Cause: Before sorting, you must specify both the Data-Range to be sorted and the Primary-Key. At least one of these is not defined.

Solution: From the Data Sort menu, press D to define the Data-Range; when this is complete, press P to define the Primary-Key.

2. You completed the sorting tutorial, but your screen does not match Fig. 6.7. For example, Scott is not associated with the correct department, credit hours, grant dollars, or sequence number. Some of the fields are not sorted. Or some of the records are not moved.

Cause: When specifying the Data-Range to be sorted, you must include all records (rows) and all fields (columns) to be sorted. You probably missed some rows or columns in the database.

Solution: The easiest solution is to start the tutorial in this chapter over again. Press / F R to retrieve the file name DATAEX and start over.

3. You have made some major mistakes in defining the sorting options but have not actually sorted the records. You'd like to start over.

Cause: You made some incorrect responses.

Solution: From the Data Sort menu

Press: R

└──── Reset

to cancel all of the sorting options.

Selecting Records from a Database

Another important data management function is **querying**. This refers to the process of searching the database for records that meet certain criteria. Some example queries of the tutorial database are to find a list of:

1. faculty who taught more than 20 credit hours

2. business faculty who obtained 0 grant dollars

3. faculty in physics and chemistry

Obviously, for the small tutorial database, these are easy to locate, but try to imagine a large database with thousands of records.

Press

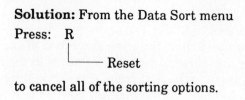

/ D Q

└── Query

└── Data

to access the 1-2-3 **Data Query** menu (Fig. 6.10). Press ⊟ to highlight each of the menu options and read the description on line 3 of the control panel to become familiar with this menu. This is another "sticky" menu. Press

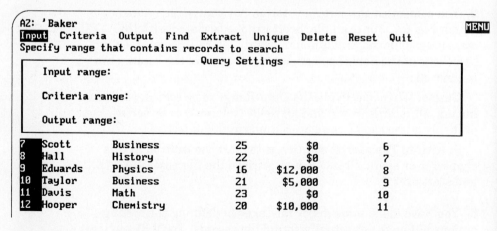

Figure 6.10 Line 2 lists the menu choices on the Data Query menu. With Release 2.2 the current query settings are displayed in a table overlaying the worksheet.

136

Q
└── Quit

to return to READY mode.

> **Keystroke Summary: Access the Data Query menu**
>
> Press: / D Q
>   │   └── Query
>   └── Data
>
> Select: *query options*
>
> Press: Q
>   └── Quit

Preparing the Worksheet for a Query

Before you can use the query options, the worksheet must be organized as a database and set up to handle the desired query. This section describes the query setup. Generally, a query has two parts: a **criterion** for selecting records and the **information desired** from the selected records. Both of these are defined in a blank area of the worksheet outside of the area that contains the database.

To illustrate these ideas, you'll set up the worksheet to answer the following query:

> "Find the name and grant dollars of each faculty member in the business department with a grant of more than 0 dollars."

The criteria for selecting records are that the faculty member be in the business department and have obtained a grant. The information desired from the selected records is the name of the faculty member and grant dollars obtained.

First, define the criteria for selecting records in the blank area of the worksheet beneath the database. Each criterion is defined by placing the field name in a cell above the acceptable values. To define the criterion DEPART-MENT = Business, position the cell pointer to cell A14 and type the field name

DEPARTMENT

as a label. Press ⏎. Move the cell pointer down one to cell A15 and type the acceptable value

Business

Press ⏎. If these two cells are defined as a criterion range, all records with DEPARTMENT = Business will be selected.

	A	B	C	D	E	F
1	NAME	DEPARTMENT	CREDIT HRS	GRANT DOLRS	SEQUENCE NO	
2	Baker	Business	24	$0	1	
3	Troy	Math	23	$0	2	
4	Smith	Math	17	$30,000	3	
5	Waller	Physics	16	$15,000	4	
6	Miller	Business	19	$8,000	5	
7	Scott	Business	25	$0	6	
8	Hall	History	22	$0	7	
9	Edwards	Physics	16	$12,000	8	
10	Taylor	Business	21	$5,000	9	
11	Davis	Math	23	$0	10	
12	Hooper	Chemistry	20	$10,000	11	
13						
14	DEPARTMENT	GRANT DOLRS				
15	Business	0				

Figure 6.11 Cells in range address A14..B15 specify the criteria for selecting records from the worksheet database. Cells A14 and A15 indicate that the DEPARTMENT must be Business, and cells B14 and B15 indicate that the GRANT DOLRS must be greater than 0.

Defining the second criterion, GRANT DOLRS > 0, is a little more complicated. Position the cell pointer to cell B14 and type

    GRANT DOLRS

Press ⏎. In this case, there are many acceptable values (any amount above 0). To handle this, move the cell pointer to B15, type the expression

    +D2>0

and press ⏎ (Fig. 6.11). D2 is the cell address of GRANT DOLRS in the first record of the database. D2 will vary as each record of the database is tested for selection. +D2>0 is called a logical expression. It is False (value = 0) if the value in cell D2 is less than or equal to 0 and is True (value = 1) if the value in cell D2 is greater than 0. All records producing a True value will be selected during the query. Thus if cells B14 and B15 are defined as the criterion range, all records with GRANT DOLRS > 0 will be selected. Later in the tutorial, you'll select all four cells, A14..B15, as the criterion range; this implies that both critera must be met before the record is selected.

Writing selection criteria is a complicated process. The reader is referred to the 1-2-3 Reference Manual under the heading "Writing Criteria" for more complex situations.

Second, define the information required from the selected records. In the tutorial query, this is the fields NAME and GRANT DOLRS. These field

	A	B	C	D	E	F
1	NAME	DEPARTMENT	CREDIT HRS	GRANT DOLRS	SEQUENCE NO	
2	Baker	Business	24	$0	1	
3	Troy	Math	23	$0	2	
4	Smith	Math	17	$30,000	3	
5	Waller	Physics	16	$15,000	4	
6	Miller	Business	19	$8,000	5	
7	Scott	Business	25	$0	6	
8	Hall	History	22	$0	7	
9	Edwards	Physics	16	$12,000	8	
10	Taylor	Business	21	$5,000	9	
11	Davis	Math	23	$0	10	
12	Hooper	Chemistry	20	$10,000	11	
13						
14	DEPARTMENT	GRANT DOLRS				
15	Business	0				
16						
17	NAME	GRANT DOLRS				

Figure 6.12 Cells in range address A17..B17 specify that the NAME and GRANT DOLRS of selected faculty members are to be extracted from the database.

names are entered in adjacent columns of a blank area of the worksheet with plenty of space below. Type

     NAME

in cell A17. Press ⏎ and type

     GRANT DOLRS

in cell B17. Press ⏎ (Fig. 6.12). If these cells are selected as the output range, the name and grant dollars of all records meeting the selection criteria will be displayed below these labels.

Defining the Query Data Range

Now that the worksheet is set up to answer a query, return to the Data Query menu; press / D Q. The first step is to define the range address containing the worksheet database. Press

    I
    └── Input

Respond to the prompt

    Enter input range: B17

by pointing to the range address A1..E12 (Fig. 6.13). The anchor cell is free and may be fixed at A1 by pressing . (period). Press ⏎. With Release 2.2 the input range A1..E2 will be displayed in the query settings table.

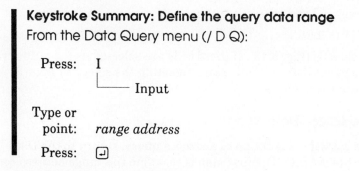

```
E12: 11                                                          POINT
Enter input range: A1..E12

          A           B           C           D           E          F
1   NAME          DEPARTMENT  CREDIT HRS  GRANT DOLRS SEQUENCE NO
2   Baker         Business          24          $0          1
3   Troy          Math              23          $0          2
4   Smith         Math              17     $30,000          3
5   Waller        Physics           16     $15,000          4
6   Miller        Business          19      $8,000          5
7   Scott         Business          25          $0          6
8   Hall          History           22          $0          7
9   Edwards       Physics           16     $12,000          8
10  Taylor        Business          21      $5,000          9
11  Davis         Math              23          $0         10
12  Hooper        Chemistry         20     $10,000         11
13
14  DEPARTMENT    GRANT DOLRS
15  Business                0
16
17  NAME          GRANT DOLRS
```

Figure 6.13 The Input range address includes the field names and the database records.

It is important to note that for Querying, the range address includes both the database records and the field names, while for Sorting, only the database records are included.

> **Keystroke Summary: Define the query data range**
> From the Data Query menu (/ D Q):
>
> Press: I
>   └── Input
>
> Type or
>   point: *range address*
>
> Press:

Defining the Criterion Range

The next step is to specify the range address that contains the criteria for selecting records from the database. Press

C
└── Criterion

POINT to the range address A14..B15 containing the selection criteria (Fig. 6.14) and press ⏎.

140

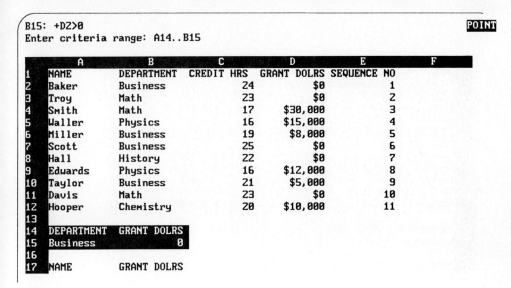

```
B15: +D2>0                                              POINT
Enter criteria range: A14..B15

        A           B          C          D          E          F
1   NAME        DEPARTMENT  CREDIT HRS  GRANT DOLRS SEQUENCE NO
2   Baker       Business        24         $0           1
3   Troy        Math            23         $0           2
4   Smith       Math            17      $30,000         3
5   Waller      Physics         16      $15,000         4
6   Miller      Business        19       $8,000         5
7   Scott       Business        25         $0           6
8   Hall        History         22         $0           7
9   Edwards     Physics         16      $12,000         8
10  Taylor      Business        21       $5,000         9
11  Davis       Math            23         $0          10
12  Hooper      Chemistry       20      $10,000         11
13
14  DEPARTMENT  GRANT DOLRS
15  Business              0
16
17  NAME        GRANT DOLRS
```

Figure 6.14 The Criterion range address specifies the criteria to be used by the query program to select records from the database.

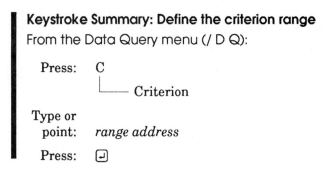

Keystroke Summary: Define the criterion range

From the Data Query menu (/ D Q):

Press: C
           └── Criterion

Type or
point: *range address*

Press: ⏎

Viewing Selected Records

Now you can view the records from the database that meet the selection criteria specified. Press

F
└── Find

and the first record in the database meeting the selection criteria will be highlighted (Fig. 6.15). Note that faculty member Miller is the first Business faculty member with a grant. Press ⬇ to highlight the next selected record, Taylor. Press ⬇ again and you'll hear a beep indicating there are no more records meeting the criterion. Use ⬆ and ⬇ to move up and down the database between selected records. When you are finished, press ⏎.

	A	B	C	D	E	F
1	NAME	DEPARTMENT	CREDIT HRS	GRANT DOLRS	SEQUENCE NO	
2	Baker	Business	24	$0	1	
3	Troy	Math	23	$0	2	
4	Smith	Math	17	$30,000	3	
5	Waller	Physics	16	$15,000	4	
6	Miller	Business	19	$8,000	5	
7	Scott	Business	25	$0	6	
8	Hall	History	22	$0	7	
9	Edwards	Physics	16	$12,000	8	
10	Taylor	Business	21	$5,000	9	
11	Davis	Math	23	$0	10	
12	Hooper	Chemistry	20	$10,000	11	
13						
14	DEPARTMENT	GRANT DOLRS				
15	Business	0				
16						
17	NAME	GRANT DOLRS				

Figure 6.15 The Find option highlights database records that satisfy the selection criteria. Press ⬆ and ⬇ to move between selected records.

Keystroke Summary: View selected records

From the Data Query menu (/ D Q):

Press: F
     └── Find

Press: ⬆ or ⬇

Press: ⏎

Extracting Records

1-2-3 also provides the capability to list certain fields of the selected records in a separate area of the worksheet. This way, the selected records are grouped together and may be printed.

First, press

O
└── Output

to define the fields to be extracted. POINT to the range address A17..B17 (Fig. 6.16) and press ⏎.

Then press

E
└── Extract

142

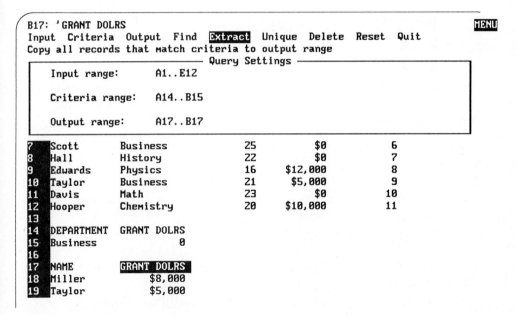

```
B17: 'GRANT DOLRS                                                    POINT
Enter output range: A17..B17

       A          B          C          D          E          F
1   NAME       DEPARTMENT  CREDIT HRS  GRANT DOLRS SEQUENCE NO
2   Baker      Business       24          $0           1
3   Troy       Math           23          $0           2
4   Smith      Math           17       $30,000         3
5   Waller     Physics        16       $15,000         4
6   Miller     Business       19        $8,000         5
7   Scott      Business       25          $0           6
8   Hall       History        22          $0           7
9   Edwards    Physics        16       $12,000         8
10  Taylor     Business       21        $5,000         9
11  Davis      Math           23          $0          10
12  Hooper     Chemistry      20       $10,000        11
13
14  DEPARTMENT GRANT DOLRS
15  Business        0
16
17  NAME       GRANT DOLRS
```

Figure 6.16 The Output range address specifies the fields to be copied from the selected records in the database.

to extract the given fields from the selected records. They are displayed beneath the field names in the database format (Fig. 6.17). You must be sure that there is sufficient space below the field names to handle the extracted records.

```
B17: 'GRANT DOLRS                                                    MENU
Input  Criteria  Output  Find  Extract  Unique  Delete  Reset  Quit
Copy all records that match criteria to output range
                        ─── Query Settings ───
    Input range:      A1..E12

    Criteria range:   A14..B15

    Output range:     A17..B17

7   Scott      Business       25          $0           6
8   Hall       History        22          $0           7
9   Edwards    Physics        16       $12,000         8
10  Taylor     Business       21        $5,000         9
11  Davis      Math           23          $0          10
12  Hooper     Chemistry      20       $10,000        11
13
14  DEPARTMENT GRANT DOLRS
15  Business        0
16
17  NAME       GRANT DOLRS
18  Miller       $8,000
19  Taylor       $5,000
```

Figure 6.17 The Extract option makes a copy of the selected fields of the selected records beneath the field names specified in the Output range address.

Other Query Options

This completes the formal tutorial in this chapter. However, before leaving the Data Query menu, you might wish to explore the menu options Unique and Delete on your own. The Unique option is identical to Extract except that, if the database contains any duplicate records, only one copy is extracted. You can test this by duplicating the Miller record in the database and comparing the results with Extract and Unique.

The Delete option is used to remove the selected records from the database. Try this option also.

What Can Go Wrong?

1. You pressed F (for Find) or E (for Extract), the computer beeped, and nothing happened.

Cause: Before selecting records with Find, you must specify the Input range and the Criterion range. For Extract, you must also specify the Output range. One of of these has not been specified.

Solution: From the Data Query menu, press I to define the Input range, C to define the Criterion range, and O to define the Output range.

2. The Find and Extract option are not selecting the records expected in the tutorial.

Cause: This is probably due to one of the following reasons: you did not include the field names in the Input range, you did not include both criteria A14..B15 in the Criterion range, or you misspelled one of the field names.

Solution: Check the range addresses specified in the query settings table. Check the spelling of field names in the Criterion range and the Output range. Make corrections as required.

3. You have made some major mistakes in defining the query options and would like to start over.

Cause: You made some incorrect responses.

Solution: From the Data Query menu

Press: R

           └── Reset

to cancel all of the querying settings.

Other Data Features

This section provides a brief introduction to some additional data features that you might wish to explore on your own. Though these features are all relatively easy to use, some require knowledge of mathematics and statistics to use properly.

Database Functions

In Chapter 4, you were introduced to 1-2-3's library of functions, in particular the statistical functions. Each of these has a corresponding function that applies to selected records of a database. For example, corresponding to @SUM, which sums the numeric values in a given range, is @DSUM, which sums the numeric values of a particular field for all selected records. In the database tutorial example, to sum the grant dollars obtained by all Business faculty, enter the function

       @DSUM(A1..E12,3,A14..B15)

The first argument, A1..E12, specifies the Input range of the worksheet database, and the third argument, A14..B15, specifies the Criterion range for selecting records. The second argument specifies the offset number of the column whose values will be summed if a record matches the criteria. Field 1 has an offset of 0, field 2 an offset of 1, and so on.

Use the tutorial worksheet to experiment with the database statistical functions. They all use the same arguments as @DSUM.

Other Options from the Data menu (/ D)

The options introduced below perform certain mathematical or statistical calculations on a set of data defined in a worksheet. To try these, you'll probably want to erase the tutorial worksheet (/ W E Y) and use the 1-2-3 Reference Manual to create a set of data appropriate for each calculation.

1. *Calculate frequency distribution:* Given a set of numeric values and a set of bins, 1-2-3 counts the number of values within each bin. (Distribution)

2. *Perform matrix operations:* Multiply or invert a matrix of values specified on the worksheet. (Matrix)

3. *Linear regression calculations:* Calculate the parameters of a linear regression model involving up to 16 independent variables. (Regression)

Summary

Function	Reference or Keystrokes	Page
Database terminology	—	127
Database worksheet	—	126
Data sequence entry	/ D F, range address, ⏎, starting number, ⏎, step size, ⏎, stopping number, ⏎	129
Query, access menu	/ D Q	136
Query, define criterion range	(/ D Q) C, range address, ⏎	140
Query, define data	(/ D Q) I, range address, ⏎	139
Query, define extraction fields	—	138
Query, define selection criteria	—	137
Query, extract selected records	(/ D Q) O, range address, ⏎, E	142
Query, view selected records	(/ D Q) F, ↓ or ↑, ⏎	141
Sort, access menu	/ D S	131
Sort, define data	(/ D S) D, range address, ⏎	132
Sort, define key	(/ D S) P or S, range address, ⏎, A or D, ⏎	133
Sort, perform	(/ D S) G	134

Self-Test

1. In a worksheet database, a worksheet column is used for each _____ and a row is used for each _____. The first row of the database contains _____ for each field.

2. For the number sequence 3, 7, 11, 15, 19, 23 indicate the

   a. Start value: _____

   b. Step value: _____

   c. Stop value: _____

3. Press _____ to enter the number sequence 3, 7, 11, 15, 19, 23 in cells A1 through A6.

4. _____ is the process of placing database records in a particular order.

5. Press _____ from the Data Sort menu to define the database records to be sorted. The fields are in columns A and B, the field names in row 5, and the records in rows 6 to 58.

6. The first column (or field) used to order database records is called the _____ , and the column used to order records with equal values in the first column is called the _____ .

7. Type _____ in response to the prompt Sort order (A or D) to order records from highest to lowest value.

8. After defining the records to be sorted and the keys to be used, press _____ from the Data Sort menu to order the records and return to READY mode.

9. _____ is the process of selecting database records that meet certain criteria.

10. Consider the following query on the tutorial database: "Find the name and department of all faculty teaching more than 19 credit hours"

   a. State the criteria for selecting records: _____

   b. Define the criteria on the worksheet by typing _____ in a blank cell and typing _____ in the cell beneath.

   c. State the information desired from the query: _____

11. The query data range includes the database records to be sorted and the _____ .

12. Press _____ from the Data Query menu to define the criterion range. Three criteria are specified in columns B, C, and D and rows 12 and 13 of the worksheet.

13. Use the Data Query menu choice _____ to highlight the selected records in the worksheet database, and use the Data Query menu choice _____ to copy certain fields from these records to a separate area of the worksheet.

Exercises

1. Print copies of Figs. 6.4, 6.7, and 6.17 and submit them to your instructor.

2. Retrieve the database tutorial worksheet and sort the records as follows:

   a. Alphabetical by instructor

   b. From fewest to most credit hours taught

   Submit a printed copy of each ordered database.

3. Retrieve the database tutorial worksheet and design it to answer the following query:

   "Find the name and grant dollars obtained of all faculty who taught more than 20 credit hours."

   List the required information and submit a printed copy of the worksheet that includes the criteria specification and the listed information.

7

Other Useful Features

This chapter introduces the 1-2-3 features and commands that allow you to:

- freeze column or row labels on the screen
- view separate portions of a worksheet on the screen
- create keystroke macros
- use 1-2-3 add-ins

Overview

This chapter completes the 1-2-3 tutorial by covering four particularly useful features. The first two features are helpful in dealing with a worksheet that contains more rows and/or columns than will fit on a single screen. This is usually the case with most realistic applications. One feature (Titles) freezes certain rows and columns on the screen during scrolling. The other (Windows) allows two separate portions of the worksheet to appear on the screen simultaneously.

The third feature, **macros**, provides 1-2-3 users the ability to write programs to automate their work. Using macros is a relatively complicated subject requiring programming skills. The tutorial introduces the basic concepts involved using simple examples. To master this subject, the interested reader should read the 1-2-3 Reference Manual or other books that specifically address the topic of macros.

Finally, you will be introduced to the subject of **add-ins**. Add-ins are programs that may be added to 1-2-3 to provide additional capabilities or features. Release 2.2 provides a menu option to access these programs.

For this tutorial, you will modify the graph worksheet to project eight quarters into the future (Fig. 7.1). This expanded worksheet has too many columns to fit on the display screen and will be used to illustrate the Titles and Windows features. Develop the worksheet as follows.

1. Retrieve the graph worksheet from disk under the file name GRAPHEX. (/ F R)

2. Copy the cell contents for quarters 1 to 4 (B2..E9) to columns F through I (F2..I9). (/ C)

3. Edit the new column headings to read: (F2)

   F2: "QTR 5

   G2: "QTR 6

   H2: "QTR 7

   I2: "QTR 8

4. Enter sales forecasts for the new quarters as follows:

   F3: 120

   G3: 190

   H3: 100

   I3: 110

5. Save the worksheet using the file name LARGEX. (/F S)

I3: 110					READY
	D	**E**	**F**	**G**	**H**	**I**

	D	E	F	G	H	I
1						
2	QTR 3	QTR 4	QTR 5	QTR 6	QTR 7	QTR 8
3	150	80	120	190	100	110
4						
5	$750	$400	$600	$950	$500	$550
6						
7	$100	$100	$100	$100	$100	$100
8	$450	$240	$360	$570	$300	$330
9	$550	$340	$460	$670	$400	$430

Figure 7.1 When you add QTR 5 through QTR 8 to the graphing tutorial worksheet, it no longer fits on the display screen.

Freezing Row Labels and Column Headings

Look at the screen illustrated in Fig. 7.1. Data for quarters 3–8 are displayed, but without the row labels visible, you don't know what the numbers represent. Using the Titles option on the Worksheet menu, you can freeze the labels in column A so that they do not scroll off the screen.

Position the cell pointer in column B (all columns to the left of the cell pointer will be frozen on the screen). Press

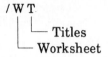

Line 2 of the control panel displays the options

```
Both Horizontal Vertical Clear
```

The Horizontal option freezes rows above the cell pointer on the screen; Vertical freezes columns to the left of the cell pointer; the Both option freezes both the rows above and columns to the left; and Clear cancels any previous settings. Press V to freeze column A.

Position the cell pointer in column I (Fig. 7.2). The screen now displays columns F through I, but column A remains frozen on the screen.

Column headings may also be frozen on the screen. Press PgDn and notice that everything scrolls off the screen. Press PgUp and position the cell pointer in row 3. Press / W T to choose the Titles option, and press H to freeze all rows above the cell pointer. Now press PgDn, and the first two rows remain on the screen (Fig. 7.3). Note that column A is no longer frozen. The Both option must be selected to freeze both columns and rows at the same time.

Press Home. Normally, this moves the cell pointer to cell A1. However, since row 1 and row 2 are fixed on the screen, the cell pointer moves to cell

I3: 110				READY
A	**F**	**G**	**H**	**I**
1 QUARTERLY REVENUE/COST P				
2	QTR 5	QTR 6	QTR 7	QTR 8
3 SALES (units)	120	190	100	110
4				
5 REVENUES ($5/unit)	$600	$950	$500	$550
6				
7 FIXED COSTS ($100/qtr)	$100	$100	$100	$100
8 VARIABLE COSTS ($3/unit)	$360	$570	$300	$330
9 TOTAL COSTS	$460	$670	$400	$430

Figure 7.2 The row labels in column A are frozen on the display screen and will not scroll off if the cursor is moved to the right.

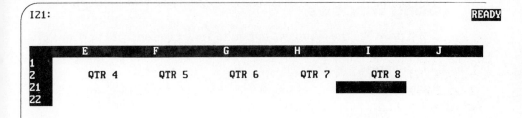

Figure 7.3 The column labels in rows 1 and 2 are frozen on the display screen and will not scroll off if the cursor is moved down.

A3. The only way to position the cell pointer in a frozen cell is to press F5 and type the desired cell address as discussed in Chapter 2. Try it. Press F5, type A1 in response to the prompt, and press ⏎ (Fig. 7.4). Row 1 and row 2 remain fixed on the screen, but a copy is made to allow the cell to be edited. To remove the duplicate rows, press PgDn to scroll them off the screen and PgUp to return to cell A3.

Complete this lesson by canceling the frozen rows. Press / W T to select the Titles option, and press C to clear the settings. Verify that the rows are no longer frozen by pressing PgDn to scroll them off the screen.

> **Keystroke Summary: Freeze rows and/or columns**
>
> Press: / W T (B or H or V or C)
>
> └────┴──────┴───── Both, Horizontal, Vertical, or
>   Clear
>
>   └── Titles
>
>   └── Worksheet

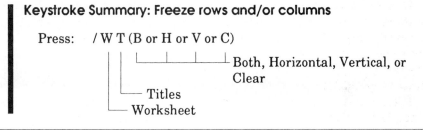

A	B	C	D	E
QUARTERLY REVENUE/COST PROJECTION:				
	QTR 1	QTR 2	QTR 3	QTR 4
QUARTERLY REVENUE/COST PROJECTION:				
	QTR 1	QTR 2	QTR 3	QTR 4
SALES (units)	100	200	150	80
REVENUES ($5/unit)	$500	$1,000	$750	$400
FIXED COSTS ($100/qtr)	$100	$100	$100	$100
VARIABLE COSTS ($3/unit)	$300	$600	$450	$240
TOTAL COSTS	$400	$700	$550	$340

Figure 7.4 If the cell pointer is moved to a frozen row or column, duplicates of the frozen rows and columns are made for editing. The duplicates may be scrolled off the screen.

Using Windows

1-2-3 provides the Windows option to view two separate portions of a large worksheet on the display screen. To illustrate, position the cell pointer in cell A11 and press

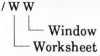

Line 2 of the control panel provides the options

```
Horizontal Vertical Sync Unsync Clear
```

The Horizontal option creates one window above the cell pointer and one below it; the Vertical option creates one window to the left of the cell pointer and one to the right. The other options will be explained shortly. Press H to create Horizontal windows (Fig. 7.5). The top window displays rows 1–10, and the bottom window displays rows 11–19.

Notice that the cell pointer is positioned in the top window. Press

F6

A10: [W24]   READY

	A	B	C	D	E
1	QUARTERLY REVENUE/COST PROJECTION:				
2		QTR 1	QTR 2	QTR 3	QTR 4
3	SALES (units)	100	200	150	80
4					
5	REVENUES ($5/unit)	$500	$1,000	$750	$400
6					
7	FIXED COSTS ($100/qtr)	$100	$100	$100	$100
8	VARIABLE COSTS ($3/unit)	$300	$600	$450	$240
9	TOTAL COSTS	$400	$700	$550	$340
10					

	A	B	C	D	E
11					
12					
13					
14					
15					
16					
17					
18					
19					

Figure 7.5 The display screen is divided into two horizontal windows at row 11 (the position of the cell pointer), each showing part of the worksheet.

	A	B	C	D	E
1	QUARTERLY REVENUE/COST PROJECTION:				
2		QTR 1	QTR 2	QTR 3	QTR 4
3	SALES (units)	150	200	150	80
4					
5	REVENUES ($5/unit)	$750	$1,000	$750	$400
6					
7	FIXED COSTS ($100/qtr)	$100	$100	$100	$100
8	VARIABLE COSTS ($3/unit)	$450	$600	$450	$240
9	TOTAL COSTS	$550	$700	$550	$340
10					

	A	B	C	D	E
1	QUARTERLY REVENUE/COST PROJECTION:				
2		QTR 1	QTR 2	QTR 3	QTR 4
3	SALES (units)	150	200	150	80
4					
5	REVENUES ($5/unit)	$750	$1,000	$750	$400
6					
7	FIXED COSTS ($100/qtr)	$100	$100	$100	$100
8	VARIABLE COSTS ($3/unit)	$450	$600	$450	$240
9	TOTAL COSTS	$550	$700	$550	$340

Figure 7.6 Cell contents may be changed or worksheet options may be selected from either window and, if visible, will be reflected in the other window.

and the cell pointer is moved to the bottom window. F6 moves the cell pointer back and forth between windows.

With the cell pointer in the bottom window, press ↑ until both windows display the same cells. Position the cell pointer on cell B3 and type

    150

to change the sales for quarter 1. Press ↵ and notice that the change is reflected in both windows (Fig. 7.6). The worksheet may be modified or edited from either window.

With the cell pointer still in the bottom window, press → until the cell pointer is in column I (Fig. 7.7). Notice that as the columns scroll left across the bottom window, they also scroll left across the top. This is called synchronous scrolling. To change to independent (or unsynchronous) scrolling, press / W W to access the Windows option menu and press

Now press F6 to move the cell pointer back to the top window. Press ← until the cell pointer is positioned in column A (Fig. 7.8). This time the columns scroll right across the top window but remain fixed in the bottom window; that is, they are not synchronized.

	D	E	F	G	H	I
1						
2	QTR 3	QTR 4	QTR 5	QTR 6	QTR 7	QTR 8
3	150	80	120	190	100	110
4						
5	$750	$400	$600	$950	$500	$550
6						
7	$100	$100	$100	$100	$100	$100
8	$450	$240	$360	$570	$300	$330
9	$550	$340	$460	$670	$400	$430
10						

	D	E	F	G	H	I
1						
2	QTR 3	QTR 4	QTR 5	QTR 6	QTR 7	QTR 8
3	150	80	120	190	100	110
4						
5	$750	$400	$600	$950	$500	$550
6						
7	$100	$100	$100	$100	$100	$100
8	$450	$240	$360	$570	$300	$330
9	$550	$340	$460	$670	$400	$430

Figure 7.7 With the horizontal windows, the columns may scroll synchronously across the screen.

	A	B	C	D	E
1	QUARTERLY REVENUE/COST PROJECTION:				
2		QTR 1	QTR 2	QTR 3	QTR 4
3	SALES (units)	150	200	150	80
4					
5	REVENUES ($5/unit)	$750	$1,000	$750	$400
6					
7	FIXED COSTS ($100/qtr)	$100	$100	$100	$100
8	VARIABLE COSTS ($3/unit)	$450	$600	$450	$240
9	TOTAL COSTS	$550	$700	$550	$340
10					

	D	E	F	G	H	I
1						
2	QTR 3	QTR 4	QTR 5	QTR 6	QTR 7	QTR 8
3	150	80	120	190	100	110
4						
5	$750	$400	$600	$950	$500	$550
6						
7	$100	$100	$100	$100	$100	$100
8	$450	$240	$360	$570	$300	$330
9	$550	$340	$460	$670	$400	$430

Figure 7.8 By selecting the Unsync option, the columns may scroll independently in each horizontal window.

Complete this section by returning to a single screen. Press / W W to access the Windows options and press

C
└── Clear

to remove the second window.

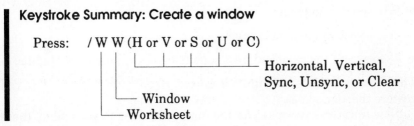

Keystroke Summary: Create a window

Press: / W W (H or V or S or U or C)

Horizontal, Vertical, Sync, Unsync, or Clear

Window

Worksheet

Introducing Macros

One of the most powerful features of 1-2-3 is macros. A **macro** is basically a set of instructions, like a computer program, to perform a particular task. The instructions in a macro are made up of keystrokes that perform 1-2-3 commands. The instructions are stored in a blank area of the worksheet and executed by a single keystroke combination. Macros are useful in several areas, saving keystrokes in commonly performed functions, eliminating the need to remember the keystrokes required to do certain tasks, and making 1-2-3 easier for the novice to use.

Creating and using macros is a three-step process:

1. Use a blank area of the worksheet to list the keystrokes required to perform the desired function.

2. Assign a name to the area of the worksheet containing the list of keystrokes (names consist of the slash character (\) followed by a single letter of the alphabet (A–Z), for example \A).

3. Execute the macro by holding down Alt *and* pressing the letter of the macro name, for example, Alt *and* A.

To save the macro, simply save the worksheet as usual. Any macros defined in the worksheet are also saved.

The tutorial illustrates this process by creating, naming, and executing a macro to erase the contents of a highlighted cell.

Defining Macro Keystrokes

The first step in defining a macro is to recall or figure out the exact keystrokes required to perform the function. It's a good idea to step through the process and write *each* keystroke down as you press it. Begin the tutorial by erasing cell B3 and recording the keystrokes used. Position the cell pointer on cell B3 (don't count these keystrokes; you'll write the macro assuming that the cell pointer is already highlighting the cell to be erased). Four keystrokes are now required. Press these to verify:

- / to access 1-2-3 menu system
- R to select Range menu option
- E to select Erase menu option
- ⏎ to accept the range address consisting of the single highlighted cell

The sales estimate of 150 units is erased. Reenter the value 150 in cell B3 to restore the worksheet.

Now that the keystrokes for the macro are clear in your mind, these must be entered *as a label* in a blank worksheet cell. Position the cell pointer to cell B11 and type

'/RE~

Press ⏎ (Fig. 7.9). The ' is a label-prefix character to indicate that the following keystrokes are to be entered as a label. Without this character, when you type /, the menu system will be activated and the keystrokes will not be entered in the cell. The remaining characters represent the four keystrokes required to erase a cell. As usual, R and E may be uppercase or lowercase, since they represent menu selections. Tilde (~) is a special character used to represent the ⏎ key in a macro. (See Fig. 7.10 for ways to represent other

---

B11: '/RE~   READY

	A	B	C	D	E
1	QUARTERLY REVENUE/COST PROJECTION:				
2		QTR 1	QTR 2	QTR 3	QTR 4
3	SALES (units)	150	200	150	80
4					
5	REVENUES ($5/unit)	$750	$1,000	$750	$400
6					
7	FIXED COSTS ($100/qtr)	$100	$100	$100	$100
8	VARIABLE COSTS ($3/unit)	$450	$600	$450	$240
9	TOTAL COSTS	$550	$700	$550	$340
10					
11		/RE~			

Figure 7.9 Cell B11 contains a label listing the keystrokes required to erase the highlighted cell of a worksheet. The ~ character is a special symbol used to represent ⏎.

To Represent	Use the Symbol
⏎	~
→	{right}
↑	{up}
←	{left}
↓	{down}
Home	{home}
F5	{goto}
Pause for interaction	{?}

Figure 7.10 Use these symbols in macro definitions to represent the indicated key. Most of the symbols enclose a keyword in brackets. A complete list is contained in the 1-2-3 Reference Manual.

special keys.) This special character is provided because pressing the ⏎ key normally marks the completion of a cell entry.

It is not necessary (and not advised for more complex macros) to enter all the keystrokes for a macro in a single cell. You may split the macro keystrokes between cells any way you like, but they must be entered in a single column of adjacent cells followed by a blank cell. Fig. 7.11 contains alternative ways of representing the tutorial macro. All versions are acceptable.

Row	Original	Alternative 1	Alternative 2
11	/RE~	/R	/
12		/E~	R
13			E
14			~
15			

Figure 7.11 Macro keystrokes must appear in successive cells of the same column but may be subdivided as desired between the cells. Some alternative ways to enter the example macro are illustrated here. A blank cell is required to mark the end of the macro.

Naming a Macro

1-2-3 provides a menu function to assign a name to a range address. You have not used this in the tutorial; rather, range addresses have been defined by typing or pointing to obtain expressions such as A1..B12. By using the range-naming function, a name such as SALES or COSTS is assigned to a particular block of cells. Then, when prompted to enter a range address, you simply type the range name. This saves time if you refer frequently to the same range address. Assigning range names is also used to name macros.

To name the macro to erase a cell, press

```
/ R N
    │ └── Name
    └── Range
```

to access the range naming options

```
Create Delete Labels Reset Table
```

Press C to Create a range name, and you'll be prompted as follows:

```
Enter name:
```

For normal range names, you may enter any name up to 14 characters long; for macros, the name consists of two characters, slash (\) and a single letter of the alphabet (\A, \B, ... \Z). Use the letter E to identify this macro as an erasing macro. Type

\E

and press ⏎. Next, you'll be prompted to enter the range address associated with the given name:

```
Enter range address: B11..B11
```

If you're not already there, POINT to the first cell containing the macro keystrokes, B11 (Fig. 7.12), and press ⏎. This assigns the name \E to the beginning cell of the tutorial macro. When you execute this macro, 1-2-3 will perform all of the keystrokes in cells B11, B12, and so on until a blank cell in column B is encountered.

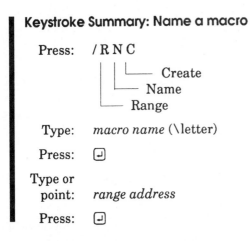

```
B11: '/RE~                                                          POINT
Enter name: \E                    Enter range: B11..B11

            A                B           C           D           E
1  QUARTERLY REVENUE/COST PROJECTION:
2                          QTR 1       QTR 2       QTR 3       QTR 4
3  SALES (units)            150         200         150          80
4
5  REVENUES ($5/unit)      $750      $1,000        $750        $400
6
7  FIXED COSTS ($100/qtr)  $100        $100        $100        $100
8  VARIABLE COSTS ($3/unit) $450       $600        $450        $240
9  TOTAL COSTS             $550        $700        $550        $340
10
11                        /RE~
```

Figure 7.12 The macro name \E is assigned to the beginning cell of the macro.

Keystroke Summary: Name a macro

Press: / R N C
                └─── Create
              └─── Name
           └─── Range

Type: *macro name* (\letter)

Press: ⏎

Type or
point: *range address*

Press: ⏎

Executing a Macro

To execute a macro, hold Alt down *and* press the letter of the macro name. To illustrate, erase the contents of cell B3 using the macro \E. Position the cell pointer over B3 and press

Alt *and* E

The keystrokes specified in the macro named \E are executed, and the contents of cell B3 are erased. Now, reenter the value 150 in cell B3.

To clarify what is happening, execute this macro again, slowly, one keystroke at a time. 1-2-3 provides a Step mode to do this. Enable Step mode by pressing

Alt *and* F2

An indicator, STEP, appears at the bottom of the screen. Position the cell pointer on cell B3 and activate the macro; press [Alt] *and* E. If you are using Release 2.2, the macro keystrokes are displayed in the lower left corner of the screen. Press

> space bar (or [↵] or any letter key)

and the first macro keystroke (/) is executed. Each time the space bar is pressed, another keystroke is executed. Trace through the remainder of this macro by pressing the space bar three more times and observe the effect of each keystroke.

When the macro is finished, turn off Step mode by pressing [Alt] *and* [F2]. Step mode is a handy feature for checking a macro. Reenter the erased value, 150, in cell B3.

Macros may be terminated before completion by pressing [Ctrl] *and* [Scroll Lock].

Keystroke Summary: Execute a macro

Press: [Alt] *and* letter of macro name

Interactive Macros

The tutorial macro erases the contents of a single highlighted cell; no interaction is involved. This macro can be generalized by allowing the user to interact and specify a range of cells to erase. 1-2-3 provides the pause command

> {?}

to do this. Simply insert this command in the macro definition at a point where interaction is desired.

To illustrate, modify the tutorial macro to allow the user to specify the range of cells to erase. Position the cell pointer on cell B11 and press [F2] to edit the macro definition. Insert the pause command between E and ~:

> '/RE{?}~

Press [↵].

Test the revised macro by erasing the range address B3..E3. Press [Alt] *and* E to execute the macro. After executing the first three keystrokes, /RE, the macro pauses for interactive input. Respond by pointing to range address B3..E3 (Fig. 7.13). CMD on line 25 indicates that 1-2-3 is executing a macro. Press [↵] to mark the end of interactive input, and the remaining keystrokes of the macro will be executed. The desired range is erased.

In general, {?} may be positioned anywhere in a macro definition. When 1-2-3 encounters this command, it stops executing the macro until you respond and press [↵]. Two of the example macros in the next section are interactive.

Before continuing, restore the erased values 150, 200, 150, and 80 in the worksheet.

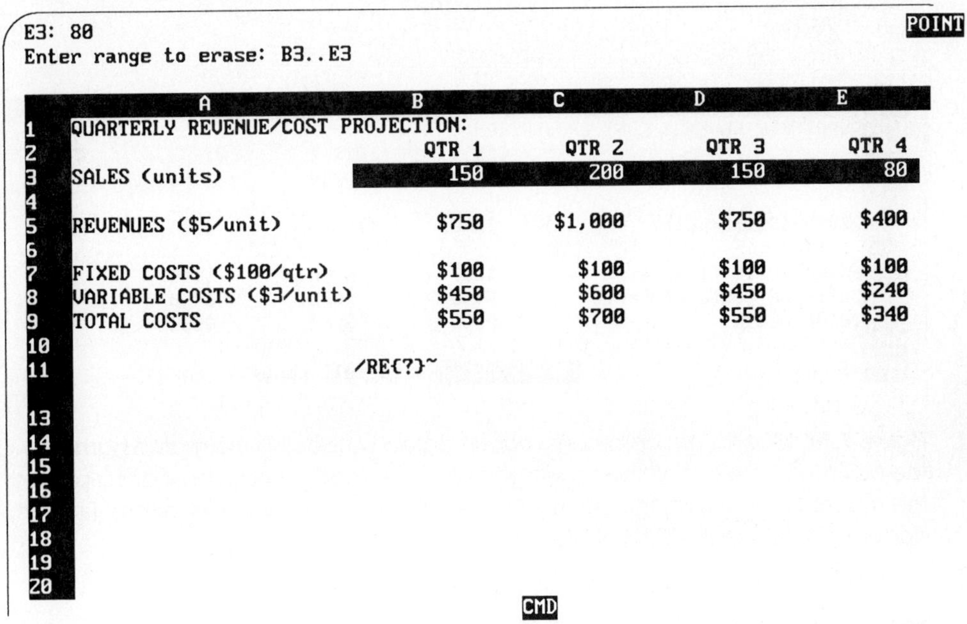

```
E3: 80
Enter range to erase: B3..E3
```

	A	B	C	D	E
1	QUARTERLY REVENUE/COST PROJECTION:				
2		QTR 1	QTR 2	QTR 3	QTR 4
3	SALES (units)	150	200	150	80
4					
5	REVENUES ($5/unit)	$750	$1,000	$750	$400
6					
7	FIXED COSTS ($100/qtr)	$100	$100	$100	$100
8	VARIABLE COSTS ($3/unit)	$450	$600	$450	$240
9	TOTAL COSTS	$550	$700	$550	$340
10					
11		/RE{?}~			
13					
14					
15					
16					
17					
18					
19					
20					

CMD

Figure 7.13 The macro pauses at {?} to allow you to point to the range address to erase. CMD on line 25 is an indicator that a macro is being executed.

Documenting a Macro

When worksheets contain complicated macros or several macros, it's a good idea to include names and descriptions of each macro as part of the worksheet. This serves as **documentation** for you or others who are using the worksheet.

Documenting is commonly done as shown in Fig. 7.14. The macro name is placed in the column to the left of the beginning cell of the macro, and a brief description is placed in the column to the right of each cell in the macro.

Document the tutorial macro. Position the cell pointer on cell A11 and type

    '\E

Press ⏎. Be sure to precede the macro name, \E, with the label-prefix character, ', or the \ part of the macro name will be treated as a label-prefix and repeat the letter E across the cell. Move the cell pointer to cell C11 and type the description

    'Erase cell range

Press ⏎, and the macro is properly documented. The documentation in cells A11 and C11 is for your information; these labels are not part of the macro.

```
B11:  '/RE{?}~                                                          READY
```

```
             A                  B              C              D              E
1  QUARTERLY REVENUE/COST PROJECTION:
2                            QTR 1          QTR 2          QTR 3          QTR 4
3  SALES (units)             150            200            150            80
4
5  REVENUES ($5/unit)        $750          $1,000          $750          $400
6
7  FIXED COSTS ($100/qtr)    $100           $100           $100           $100
8  VARIABLE COSTS ($3/unit)  $450           $600           $450           $240
9  TOTAL COSTS               $550           $700           $550           $340
10
11  \E                    /RE{?}~          Erase cell range
```

Figure 7.14 Macros are commonly documented by placing the macro name in the column to the left of the beginning cell of the macro and a brief description of the macro keystrokes in the column to the right of each cell in the macro. Proper documentation of the tutorial macro is illustrated.

Macro Names

Beginning with Release 2.2, macros may be assigned full-length range names, rather than the cryptic single-letter names described in this section. This allows more meaningful macro names. However, if a longer name is used, the macro must be executed by pressing Alt *and* F3 and then selecting the macro name from a set of available range names. This requires additional keystrokes, beyond the normal Alt *and* letter, to execute the macro. It's up to you to decide whether the benefits of longer range names are worth the additional keystrokes to execute the macro. The tutorial describes the short-cut method to be consistent across all releases of 1-2-3.

Macro Examples

The only way to learn to use macros is to create and test them. Fig. 7.15 provides four examples for the tutorial worksheet. Continue the tutorial by doing each of these, one at a time. Enter the macro into the worksheet, name it, execute it, and verify that it works. Add the documentation in the adjacent cells if you wish.

Example 1

Example macro 1 freezes the labels in column A and rows 1 and 2 of the worksheet so that they will not scroll off the screen. Enter the macro defini-

	A	B	C	D	E
11	\E	/RE{?}~	Erase cell range		
12					
13	EXAMPLE 1				
14	\T	{goto}B3~	Position cell pointer at B3		
15		/WTB	Freeze col A, row 1, and row 2		
16					
17	EXAMPLE 2				
18	\C	/WTC	Clear titles		
19					
20	EXAMPLE 3				
21	\F	/RFC	Format range of cells using currency		
22		2~	Two decimal places		
23		~	Highlighted cell only		
24					
25	EXAMPLE 4				
26	\P	/PPR	Print the worksheet		
27		{?}~	Point to desired print range		
28		GQ	Print and quit		
29					

Figure 7.15 For additional practice, add the four example macros to your worksheet. Enter the keystrokes, name the macro, execute it, and verify that it works properly.

tion in cells B14 and B15. In B14, type

> '{goto}B3~

The symbol {goto} represents [F5], the function key to move the cell pointer to a particular address. B3 is the specified address, and ~ represents the [↵] key. In B15, type

> '/WTB

to select the Worksheet option to freeze Titles. B indicates that Both columns to the left of the cell pointer and rows above the cell pointer will be frozen.

Press / R N C to create a name for this macro. Type

> \T

for the macro name and specify

> B14..B14

as the range address containing the beginning cell.

Press [Alt] *and* T to execute this macro. Make sure that it worked. Move the cell pointer to the right and down until columns and rows scroll off of the screen. Verify that column A and rows 1 and 2 remain in place.

Example 2

Example macro 2 unfreezes any rows or columns frozen on the screen. Enter this macro definition in cell B18:

'/WTC

These keystrokes call the Worksheet menu option involving Titles. C selects the option to Clear all titles.

Name this macro by pressing / R N C and typing

\C

as the macro name and

B18..B18

as the macro address.

Execute this macro by pressing [Alt] *and* C. Test it as you did Example 1. This time column A and rows 1 and 2 will scroll off the screen.

Example 3

Example macro 3 formats a cell highlighted by the cell pointer to Currency format. The user interactively specifies the number of decimal places. Organize this macro definition in three cells. In cell B21, type

'/RFC

to select the menu option to format a range of cells using the Currency format. In cell B22, type

'{?}~

to allow the user to specify the number of decimal places during the macro execution. In cell B23, type

'~

to accept the range address containing the highlighted cell.

Press / R N C to name this macro \F, and point to range address B21..B21 as the beginning cell.

To test this macro, position the cell pointer at any number on the worksheet. Press [Alt] *and* F. The macro will begin execution and pause for you to enter the number of decimal places. Type 2 and press [↵]. The macro will finish by formatting the cell to Currency with two decimal places. Execute this macro several times, each time specifying a different number of decimal places and observing the results.

Example 4

The final example macro prints an interactively specified worksheet range and returns to READY mode. This macro definition is broken down into three cells. In cell B26, type

> '/PPR

These keystrokes select the menu option to define a range to be printed. In cell B27, type

> '{?}~

so that the macro will pause and allow the user to point to the range address for printing. In cell B28, complete the macro by typing

> 'GQ

G (for Go) prints the range address, and Q (for Quit) returns to READY mode. Name this macro by pressing / R N C and typing

> \P

as the macro name and

> B26..B26

as the macro address.

Use this macro to print part of the worksheet. Press [Alt] and P. The macro will pause for you to specify the print range. Point to the range desired and press [↵]. The specified area of the worksheet will be printed, and you'll return to READY mode. Test the macro again, specifying a different print range.

What Can Go Wrong?

1. You are defining keystrokes in a worksheet cell that select a menu option. When you press these keys, the menu comes up rather than being entered in the cell as a label.

Cause: As soon as you press /, 1-2-3 goes into MENU mode.

Solution: Begin the cell entry with the label-prefix character ', so that it goes into LABEL mode first. This character is not one of the macro keystrokes.

2. You press [Alt] and a letter (A–Z), and the machine beeps without executing the macro.

Cause: 1-2-3 cannot find a range named \letter (A–Z).

Solution: Press / R N C as described above to assign an appropriate range name to the cells containing the macro definition.

3. The macro stops before completion. It is not at a point where user interaction is expected.

Cause: The macro definition is missing one or more keystrokes required to perform the given task or contains some incorrect keystrokes. A very common error is to omit a necessary ~ (or [↵]).

Solution: Press Ctrl *and* ScrollLock) to discontinue execution of the macro. Carefully check the keystrokes required and compare those with your macro definition. Look for a missing ↵ key. If you still can't find your problem, execute the macro using Step mode and compare the keystrokes executed with what you expected. Once the missing or incorrect keystrokes are identified, press Ctrl *and* ScrollLock to terminate the macro, then highlight the cell with the error and press F2 to edit the cell contents.

1-2-3 Add-Ins

Add-ins are programs written by Lotus and other software developers that provide 1-2-3 with additional capabilities. Add-ins are used from inside the normal 1-2-3 environment. Often when an add-in is invoked a new 1-2-3 menu will appear on line 2 of the control panel. Features may be selected from this menu in the same way that features are selected from the standard 1-2-3 menus illustrated in this book. In effect, the add-in becomes part of 1-2-3.

Add-ins are available for a wide variety of purposes. For example, add-ins are on the market for attaching notes to each cell entry, printing worksheets sideways across the page, creating three-dimensional graphs based on worksheet data, solving linear programming problems with the objective and constraints entered in worksheet cells, and adding additional mathematical functions for use in cell formulas.

Before Release 2.2 of 1-2-3, anyone who wished to use add-ins needed to load an add-in manager as a part of the driver set at installation. Add-ins could then be loaded during a 1-2-3 session by pressing the key combination Alt *and* F10. With Release 2.2 the add-in manager is a normal part of 1-2-3, and add-ins are loaded directly with the menu system. The tutorial describes loading add-ins using Release 2.2.

Lotus provides two add-ins with the normal purchase of 1-2-3, Release 2.2. One of the add-ins is a Macro Library Manager. This allows macros to be stored in a library file, rather than being associated with a particular worksheet as illustrated in the tutorial. By using the Library Manager you can use the same macro on several worksheets without entering it in each one. The other add-in, called Allways, provides features for formatting and printing 1-2-3 worksheets. These features allow you to format worksheets with various fonts and character sizes, variable row heights and column widths, boldfacing, underlining, horizontal and vertical lines, cell shading, and graphs. Note that Allways requires a hard disk system with at least 512K of memory.

To use an add-in, it must first be loaded into memory. To illustrate, you will load the Macro Library Manager into memory. An add-in may be loaded by using the main menu option Add-In. Press

```
/ A
  └─ Add-In
```

Line 2 of the control panel provides five options:

```
Attach Detach Invoke Clear Quit
```

Attach loads an add-in program into memory, and Detach removes it from memory. Invoke is used to execute an add-in. Clear removes all add-ins from memory, and Quit returns to READY mode. Press

> **A**

to load an add-in program. You will receive the prompt

```
Enter add-in to attach: C:\123\*.ADN
```

Add-in programs have an extension ADN. Line 3 of the control panel will list the available add-ins in your system directory. Highlight MACROMGR.ADN and press ↵. The Macro Library Manager add-in will be loaded into memory, and line 2 of the control panel will provide the options

```
No-Key 7 8 9 10
```

to assign the key combination you will use to invoke the add-in. If you choose No-Key, you will invoke the macro from the Add-In menu (/ A I). If you choose 7, 8, 9, or 10, you will invoke the macro using the key combination [Alt] *and* [F7] or [F8] or [F9] or [F10]. Press

> **7**

to assign [Alt] *and* [F7] to execute the macro. The Macro Library Manager has been loaded into memory. Press Q to Quit and return to READY mode.

To see that the add-in has been loaded, invoke the Macro Library Manager by pressing

> [Alt] *and* [F7]

Line 2 of the control panel will display the menu for the Macro Library Manager:

```
Load Save Edit Remove Name-List Quit
```

The purpose of this exercise is to illustrate how to load and invoke an add-in. The menu options of the Macro Library Manager add-in will not be discussed. Press Q to Quit and return to READY mode.

If you later decide that you do not need this add-in, you can remove it from memory. This will free some memory for other add-ins or larger worksheets. To illustrate, remove the Macro Library Manager by pressing

> / A D
>   └── Add-In
>   └── Detach

In response to the prompt

```
Enter add-in to detach:
```

highlight MACROMGR on line 3 of the control panel and press ⏎. Press Q to return to READY mode. You may verify that the add-in is gone by pressing ⒜𝗅𝗍 and ⒡𝟩. You will obtain no response.

The ability to use add-ins is an important feature of 1-2-3. It allows users of 1-2-3 to obtain additional software capabilities without 1-2-3 becoming such a large product that it will not fit in traditional PC memory limits. Add-in features may be loaded into memory as required and removed from memory when no longer needed.

Summary

Function	Reference (or keystrokes)	Page
Add-ins, invoke	(Alt) *and* (F7) or (F8) or (F9) or (F10)	167
Add-ins, load	/ A A, file name, ⏎, function key, Q	166
Add-ins, remove	/ A D, file name, ⏎	167
Macros, define	—	155
Macros, document	—	161
Macros, execute	(Alt) and letter	159
Macros, interacting	—	160
Macros, name	/ R N C, \ letter, ⏎, range address, ⏎	158
Macros, special symbols	Fig. 7.10	157
Macros, step through	(Alt) *and* (F2)	159
Macros, stop	(Ctrl) *and* (Scroll Lock)	160
Titles, columns and rows	/ W T B	150
Titles, columns only	/ W T H	150
Titles, go to title cell	(F5), cell address, ⏎	151
Titles, remove	/ W T C	151
Titles, rows only	/ W T V	150
Windows, change	(F6)	152
Windows, create side/side	/ W W V	152
Windows, create top/bottom	/ W W H	152
Windows, remove	/ W W C	155
Windows, synchronize	/ W W S	153
Windows, unsynchronize	/ W W U	153

Self-Test

1. Position the cell pointer in cell _____ to freeze the contents of columns A, B, and C and row 1 on the screen.

2. After positioning the cell pointer appropriately, press _____ to freeze the rows above the cell pointer on the screen.

3. Press _____ to move the cell pointer to a cell that is frozen on the screen.

4. Position the cell pointer in column _____ to create side-by-side windows with columns A, B, C, and D in the left window.

5. Press _____ to move the cell pointer to the other window.

6. With side-by-side windows, when the cell pointer is moved down, the rows scroll off the screen in unison.

   a. This is called _____ scrolling.

   b. Press _____ to allow the rows in each window to scroll independently.

7. A macro to erase the entire worksheet is to be entered in cell B20.

   a. Position the cell pointer on B20 and type _____ to define the keystrokes in this macro.

   b. Press _____ to name this macro \E.

   c. Press _____ to execute this macro.

8. The symbol _____ is used in a macro definition to represent the ⏎ key, and the symbol _____ is used to represent the ⊟ key.

9. Press _____ prior to executing a macro so that the macro will pause after each keystroke until you press the _____.

10. The command _____ is used in a macro definition to suspend execution of the macro until the user responds and presses ⏎.

11. Including names and descriptions of macro definitions in adjacent cells is called _____.

12. A macro definition may appear in several adjacent cells of a single _____. A _____ cell marks the end of the macro definition.

13. The name of the macro is assigned to the address of the _____ cell of the macro definition.

14. Press _____ to load add-in ALLWAYS.ADN into memory and to assign it to key combination Alt *and* F10.

Exercises

1. Print copies of Figs. 7.2, 7.8, and 7.15 and submit them to your instructor.

2. Retrieve the tutorial worksheet used in this chapter and create the display illustrated on the next page. Two windows have been created. The top window displays three example macros, and the bottom window displays projections for quarters 5 through 8. Notice that the columns are not synchronized and the bottom window has the row labels frozen on the screen. *Hint:* Rows and columns may be frozen independently in each window by using the Titles option while the cell pointer is positioned in the desired window. Press ⇧ *and* PrtSc to obtain a copy of the display to submit to your instructor.

	A	B	C	D	E
13	EXAMPLE 1				
14	\T	{goto}B3~	Position cell pointer at B3		
15		/WTB	Freeze col A, row 1, and row 2		
16					
17	EXAMPLE 2				
18	\C	/WTC	Clear titles		
19					
20	EXAMPLE 3				
21	\F	/RFC	Format range of cells using currency		
22		2~	Two decimal places		
23		~	Highlighted cell only		

	A	F	G	H	I
2		QTR 5	QTR 6	QTR 7	QTR 8
3	SALES (units)	120	190	100	110
4					
5	REVENUES ($5/unit)	$600	$950	$500	$550
6					
7	FIXED COSTS ($100/qtr)	$100	$100	$100	$100
8	VARIABLE COSTS ($3/unit)	$360	$570	$300	$330
9	TOTAL COSTS	$460	$670	$400	$430

3. Start with a blank worksheet. Define, name, test, and document macros to perform the following functions.

   a. Create a macro named \W that creates side-by-side windows in which the left window contains columns A, B, and C.

   b. Create a macro named \C that centers the label in the highlighted cell.

   c. Create a macro named \I that increases the column width of the currently highlighted column by two spaces.

   d. Create a macro named \S that enters a sequence of numbers, 1, 2, 3,..., into an interactively specified range of cells.

   Print the area of the worksheet containing these documented macro definitions.

Setup and Installation

Formatting a Floppy Disk

1. Boot DOS if necessary.

2. In response to the operating system's prompt, type one of the following commands:
   - FORMAT A: (to format a floppy disk in the A drive)
   - FORMAT B: (to format a floppy disk in the B drive)

   and press ⏎.

3. Insert a blank disk in the indicated drive and press ⏎.

4. Respond to the operating system's "format another" prompt by typing Y or N. If you type Y, you will be prompted to insert and format another blank disk.

Installing 1-2-3 on a Hard Disk System

Note: For a two-floppy-disk system, omit Steps 3–7 and make backup copies of all your disks. For Step 8, place the Install Disk in drive A.

1. Boot DOS if necessary.

2. Place the System Disk in drive A and type

   A:

and press ⏎ to make drive A the default. Then type

    INIT

and press ⏎. Follow the instructions to initialize this disk with your name and company. This step is required with Release 2.2 and later.

3. Type

    C:

to return to drive C, and type the command

    MD \123

and press ⏎ to create the directory 123 to store your program files.

4. Type the command

    MD \123DATA

and press ⏎ to create the directory 123DATA to store your worksheet files.

5. Type the command

    CD \123

and press ⏎ to move to the 123 directory.

6. Insert the System Disk in drive A, type

    COPY A:*.* C:

and press ⏎ to copy the program files from the disk to the 123 directory on your hard disk.

7. Repeat Step 6 with all disks except the Allways disks. Store the disks in a safe place.

8. Type the command

    INSTALL

and press ⏎. Carefully follow the instructions for first-time installation. You'll be asked to identify the type of monitor, the type of text printer, and the type of graphics printer attached to your system. Save this information in a driver set. The default name is 123.SET.

9. The hard disk is now ready to load 1-2-3 as described in Chapter 2.

Installing PrintGraph on a Hard Disk System

Note: If you are using a two-floppy-disk system, omit Step 2 and place the PrintGraph disk in drive A. In Step 4, specify the directory B:, and in Step 5 specify the directory A:.

1. Boot DOS if necessary.

2. Type the command

   CD \123

   and press ⏎.

3. Type the command

   PGRAPH

   and press ⏎.

4. Press

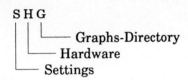

   Type

   C:\123DATA

   and press ⏎ to define the directory to store graph files.

5. Press

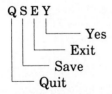

   Type

   C:\123

   and press ⏎ to define the directory containing 1-2-3 font files.

6. Press

   P
   └── Printer

   Use ⬇ to highlight the low-density version of your printer. Press ⏎.

7. Press

   Q S E Y
   │ │ │ └── Yes
   │ │ └── Exit
   │ └── Save
   └── Quit

   to save the settings and return to the DOS prompt.

8. The hard disk is now ready to print graphs as described in Appendix D.

B

1-2-3 Quick Reference

Function	Reference or Keystrokes	Page
Absolute cell address	F4	93
Add-ins, invoke	Alt *and* F7 or F8 or F9 or F10	167
Add-ins, load	/ A A, file name, ↵, function key, Q	166
Add-ins, remove	/ A D, file name, ↵	167
Boot DOS	—	12
Cell entry, formula	Formula, ↵	28
Cell entry, label	Label, ↵	21
Cell entry, number	Number, ↵	23
Cell pointer, move cursor	Fig. 2.4	18
Cell pointer, move direct	F5, cell address, ↵	20
Column width, set column	/ W C S, ⇨ or ⇦, ↵	64
Column width, set default	/ W G C, ⇨ or ⇦, ↵	62
Copy cell contents	/ C, range address FROM, ↵, range address TO, ↵	87
Database terminology	—	127
Database worksheet	—	126
Data sequence entry	/ D F, range address, ↵, starting number, ↵, step size, ↵, stopping number, ↵	129

174

Function	Reference or Keystrokes	Page
Delete columns	/ W D C, range address, ⏎	54
Delete rows	/ W D R, range address, ⏎	56
Edit cell contents	F2, Fig. 2.23	39
Erase range	/ R E, range address, ⏎	75
Erase worksheet	/ W E Y	74
Exit 1-2-3	/ Q Y	46
File names	—	36
Format options	Fixed, Currency, Percent, General, and Comma; Fig.3.21	69
Format, set default	/ W G F, format option, decimal places, ⏎	70
Format, set range	/ R F, format option, decimal places, ⏎, range address, ⏎	72
Functions, built-in	—	99
Functions, statistical	Fig. 4.26	100
Graph, access menu	/ G	110
Graph, define axis labels	(/ G O) T, X or Y, label, ⏎	119
Graph, define legend	(/ G O) L, A or B or C or D or E or F, legend, ⏎	120
Graph, define title	(/ G O) T, F or S, title, ⏎	119
Graph, define values	(/ G) A or B or C or D or E or F, range address, ⏎	111
Graph, define X values	(/ G) X, range address, ⏎	113
Graph, options menu	(/ G) O	117
Graph, select type	(/ G) T, L or B or P	114
Graph, view	(/ G) V	114
Insert columns	/ W I C, range address, ⏎	59
Insert rows	/ W I R, range address, ⏎	61
Label-prefix characters	Fig. 2.8	22
Label-prefix, set center	/ R L C, range address, ⏎	67
Label-prefix, set left	/ R L L, range address, ⏎	67
Label-prefix, set right	/ R L R, range address, ⏎	67
Load 1-2-3, floppy disk	—	14
Load 1-2-3, hard disk	—	15
Macros, define	—	155
Macros, document	—	161
Macros, execute	Alt *and* letter	159
Macros, interacting	—	160
Macros, name	/ R N C, \ letter, ⏎, range address, ⏎	158
Macros, special symbols	Fig. 7.10	157
Macros, step through	Alt *and* F2	159
Macros, stop	Ctrl *and* ScrollLock	160
Menu, access	/	31
Menu, back out	Esc	35
Menu, select method 1	→ or ←, ⏎	32
Menu, select method 2	First letter of menu option	34

Function	Reference or Keystrokes	Page
Move cell contents	/ M, range address FROM, ↵, range address TO, ↵	95
Point, complete	↵	81
Point, continue formula	Operator: + - * / ( )	85
Point, fix anchor cell	. (period)	82
Point, free anchor cell	Esc	82
Point, keys	←, →, ↑, ↓	81
Print a graph	Appendix D	179
Print a worksheet	/ P P R, range address, ↵, G, Q	43
Query, access menu	/ D Q	136
Query, define criterion range	(/ D Q) C, range address, ↵	140
Query, define data	(/ D Q) I, range address, ↵	139
Query, define extraction fields	—	138
Query, define selection criteria	—	137
Query, extract selected records	(/ D Q) O, range address, ↵, E	142
Query, view selected records	(/ D Q) F, ↓ or ↑, ↵	141
Range, definition	—	42
Range menu options	Fig. 3.19	67
Relative cell address	—	90
Retrieve file	/ F R, file name, ↵	52
Save a graph to print	(/ G) S, file name, ↵	122
Save a graph to view	/ F S, file name, ↵	121
Save a worksheet	/ F S, file name, ↵	36
Sort, access menu	/ D S	131
Sort, define data	(/ D S) D, range address, ↵	132
Sort, define key	(/ D S) P or S, range address, ↵, A or D, ↵	133
Sort, perform	(/ D S) G	134
Sticky menu	—	110
Sticky menu exit	Q	111
Titles, columns and rows	/ W T B	150
Titles, columns only	/ W T H	150
Titles, go to title cell	F5, cell address, ↵	151
Titles, remove	/ W T C	151
Titles, rows only	/ W T V	150
Undo last operation	Alt and F4	27
Windows, change	F6	152
Windows, create side/side	/ W W V	152
Windows, create top/bottom	/ W W H	152
Windows, remove	/ W W C	155
Windows, synchronize	/ W W S	153
Windows, unsynchronize	/ W W U	153
Worksheet menu options	Fig. 3.4	55

Answers to Chapter Self-Tests

Chapter 1

1. students
   tests and assignments
2. hardware
3. booting
4. memory
   secondary storage
5. in combination
6. in sequence

Chapter 2

1. mm-dd-yy
   hh.mm
2. 123
3. control panel
4. cell pointer
5. A1
   E3
6. 20
   8
7. a. ⊖
   b. PgDn
   c. Ctrl *and* ⊖

   d. Home
8. label
   number
   formula
9. label-prefix character
10. VALUE
11. \-
12. +A1+A2
13. (A1+A2)/2
14. /
15. F
16. / F S, SALES, ↵
17. F2
18. End
19. Esc
    ↵
20. a. A2.C5
    b. A1.E5
21. / P P R, A1.B5, ↵
22. / P P G from READY mode
    or simply G from print
    menu
23. / Q Y

Chapter 3

1. a. File
   b. Worksheet
   c. Range
   d. Worksheet
2. a. directory names have a \ character attached
   b. use ⊡ or ⊟ to highlight and press ⏎
3. / W D R, A3.A5, ⏎
4. +A7/12
5. / W I C, B1.C1, ⏎
6. ⊡, ⊟
7. / W G C, ⊡, ⊟, ⊟, ⏎
8. / R L C, B1.F5, ⏎
9. a. —456.83
   b. —$3,561
   c. -3,561.1
   d. ——78.3%
10. / R F F, ⏎, D2.F8, ⏎
11. / W E Y
12. / R E ⏎
13. Worksheet delete moves following columns over and Range erase does not.

Chapter 4

1. anchor
2. ⊟
   ⬆
3. . (period)
   Esc
4. cell pointer
5. ⏎
   an arithmetic operator
6. a. "TOTALS
   b. 13.45

   c. +B1/12
   d. +$A$1-3
   e. +$A$2*B1
7. B3..F3
8. F4
9. a. +C1/2
   b. (blank)
   c. +A2*3
10. @
11. arguments
12. a. 9
    b. 10
    c. 1

Chapter 5

1. spreadsheets
   graphing
   data management
2. / G
   O or / G O
3. sticky
4. 6
   1
5. A, B1.E1, ⏎
6. X, B2.E2, ⏎
7. V
8. T P
9. T F, PLOT OF QUARTERLY SALES, ⏎
10. T X, QUARTER, ⏎
11. L B, SALES, ⏎
12. S, PLOT, ⏎

Chapter 6

1. field
   record
   names
2. a. 3
   b. 4

   c. 23
3. / D F, A1.A6, ⏎, 3, ⏎, 4, ⏎, 23, ⏎
4. Sorting
5. D, A6.B58, ⏎
6. primary-key
   secondary-key
7. D
8. G
9. Querying
10. a. credit hours > 19
    b. CREDIT HRS +C2>19
    c. name and department
11. field names
12. C, B12.D13, ⏎
13. Find Extract

Chapter 7

1. D2
2. / W T H
3. F5
4. E
5. F6
6. a. synchronous
   b. / W W U
7. a. '/WEY
   b. / R N C, \E, ⏎, ⏎
   c. Alt and E
8. ~
   {right}
9. Alt and F2 space bar
10. {?}
11. documentation
12. column
    blank
13. first
14. / A A, ALLWAYS.ADN, ⏎, 7, Q

Printing Graphs

Note: Before printing graphs, make sure that PrintGraph is installed as described in Appendix A.

Printing Graphs Using a Hard Disk System

Note: For a two-floppy-disk system, omit Step 2 and place the PrintGraph Disk backup in drive A and the data disk containing the graph to be printed in drive B.

1. Boot DOS if necessary.

2. Type the command

   CD \123

   and press ⏎ to move to the 123 directory.

3. Type the command

   PGRAPH

   and press ⏎.

4. Press

I
└── Image-Select

Use to highlight the file containing the graph you wish to print. Press 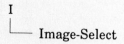.

5. Press

G
└── Go

to begin printing.

6. Press

E Y
│ └── Yes
└── Exit

to exit the PrintGraph program.